P9-BHW-701

Creative Carving of Fruits & Vegetables

ISBN: 978-81-7436-170-7

Photographs: Deepak Budhraja

Second edition
Published in India by
Roli Books in arrangement with
Roli & Janssen BV, The Netherlands

M-75, Greater Kailash-II (Market)
New Delhi-110 048, India.
Ph: ++91 11 29212271, 29212782, Fax: ++91 11 29217185
Email: roli@vsnl.com, Website: rolibooks.com

Design: Sneha Pamneja

Printed and bound in Singapore

Creative Carving of Fruits & Vegetables

Kikky Sihota

Photographs:
Deepak Budhraja

Lustre Press
Roli Books

Contents

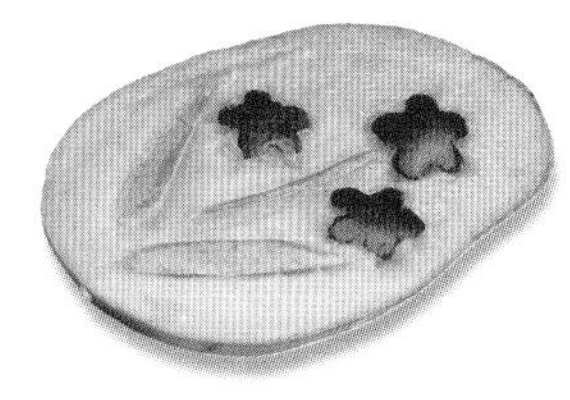

Introduction

The beautiful colours, textures and flavours of fruits and vegetables that our bountiful planet offers us are limitless. Our very existence depends on these wonderful gifts of nature, and we have learnt over the ages ingenious and attractive ways of preparing them in an attractive and appetising manner. This book will teach you, step-by-step, to create a host of wonderful shapes with these, with just a flick of the knife. It is amazing what just a little notch here or a groove there can achieve! All the methods given here are as easy as pie, and eye-catching as well. The addition of salads and desserts help balance the 'heavy dishes', and add zest and variety to the meal.

Working with fruits and vegetables is fun, but one has be very careful, as they are a delicate medium. Fruits tend to discolour very quickly, and need to be rubbed with lemon juice to preserve their original colour.

The cardinal rules of fruit and vegetable carving are – always use a small, sharp knife; ripe, firm fruits; and unblemished vegetables of good quality.

Most fruits and vegetables can be easily shaped into a variety of flowers – the ones with the same shape and texture can be carved in a similar fashion. Oval or long fruits can be transformed into boats, lamps and lanterns, and the round ones into bowls, baskets, and other innovative forms. Give free rein to your imagination, and with this book as your guide, you will be able to effortlessly carve intricate display pieces and table centres. All that is needed is ample time and a bit of patience! And to keep your creations fresh for hours, cover them with muslin soaked in cold water and wrung out. They will emerge vibrantly fresh and visually appealing – a treat for the eyes.

Keep the final product simple. If you make complicated fillings with too many ingredients, you smother the taste of the fruit or vegetable. And remember, nothing brings out the true flavour of a fruit or vegetable like lemon juice. Add a dash of lemon juice, and you will be amazed at the difference it makes!

Happy carving!

1
2
3
4
5
6
7
8
9
10
11
12
13
14
CRYSTAL

Fruit & Vegetable Carving Equipment

1. A grapefruit knife is ideal for scooping out round fruits to make baskets and containers.
2. Nowadays, a variety of knives for fancy cutting are available. One can make innovative shapes with those with 'v' or zigzag blades.
3. Melon ballers in two sizes
4. The most vital piece of equipment needed is a small, sharp knife. It gives one total control over the carving – as fruits and vegetables are soft in texture, this is of great importance.
5. A corer is essential for de-seeding apples and pears and scooping out cucumber and zucchini to make canapé shells.
6. A good medium-sized knife is also essential, especially for cutting or slicing bigger fruits.
7. A peeler is required for fruits that have to be skinned before use.
8. A fine mesh grater or lemon 'zester' is extremely useful.
9. A chef's knife easily slices through large or hard-to-cut fruits like watermelons and pineapples.
10. A pair of stainless steel scissors
11. A mandolin cutter to slice or julienne neatly and uniformly.
12. Small flower and fancy-shaped cutters.
13. A good chopping board
14. Toothpicks and satay sticks. – guests should be cautioned if these are used for individual presentations.
15. X-acto or linoleum knives are used to carve simple and attractive designs on tough rinds like that of pumpkin and watermelon.
16. An assortment of bowls
17. Food colours and paint brushes

Numbers 15, 16 and 17 are not shown.

Fruits

Apple

The legendary 'forbidden' fruit that is supposed to have led to the loss of innocence and the subsequent propagation of the human race, the apple has been known and loved since time immemorial. 'An apple a day keeps the doctor away' is an old adage we have all grown up with. Rich in calcium and phosphorous, it is perhaps the most popular and well-known fruit in the world. There are few fruits which can rival a luscious, crunchy apple in taste.

✻ APPLE SWAN

1. Take a firm, ripe, red apple. Cut off a slice from one side, about halfway between the core and the outer edge, to make a flat base. Apply lemon juice to prevent it from getting discoloured. Keep aside.

2. With a small, sharp knife, cut out a small wedge from one side. Make two cuts on both sides of the wedge,

2

3 

Carefully ease out the slices. Apply lemon juice and telescope them back together again. Repeat the entire procedure on the other side of the apple. You have now made wings on both sides of the fruit.

4. From the first reserved slice, carve out the head and neck of a swan.

about 1/8″ away from the outer edge, and cut out another slice.

3. You have just cut a slice outside a slice. Repeat this process twice. Do not remove the slices, but make sure that they are cut through. You now have four slices that telescope into each other.

5

5. Place the apple flat on it base, and position the neck of the swan on the top towards the stem end (the broader side of the apple).

6. Now open out the telescoping slices half an inch apart and place them back in the spaces on either side to give a feather-like effect.

7. Your apple swan is now ready.

8. The apple feathers created for the body of the swan can also be used separately as attractive garnishes for salads and savouries.

8

✻ SANGARITA SALAD

Ingredients

2 apples, peeled, cored, thinly sliced
2 oranges, peeled, segmented, pitted
4 leaves of lettuce, trimmed from the stem end
250 gm cottage cheese
1 tsp orange rind, grated

For the dressing:

1/2 cup orange juice
1/4 cup oil
1 tsp orange rind
1 tbsp lemon juice
salt to taste
sugar to taste
1/2 tsp black pepper
2 tsp paprika flakes
1 tbsp basil, chopped

For the garnish:

4 apple feathers (steps 1-3, pp 12-13)
a few basil leaves
2 tbsp preserved orange rind slivers (see p. 29)

Method

1. Place the lettuce leaves on one side of a salad plate.
2. Mix the orange rind with the cottage cheese and place it on the middle of the lettuce leaf.
3. Arrange the orange segments alternately with the apple slices on one side of the lettuce. Keep cool.
4. For the dressing, mix all the dressing ingredients together and store in a bottle. Discard any seeds in the paprika flakes before you add it.
5. Before serving, shake the dressing vigorously and pour it over the salad.
6. Garnish with the apple feathers, basil leaves and orange slivers.

Avocado

Avocado is commonly grown in central and South America, Africa and some parts of the Middle East. It has an elongated pear shape and is sometimes called an alligator pear. Once mature, the skin either remains a shiny dark green, or becomes knobbly and purplish. The flesh inside is a creamy green, with a buttery texture. For table use, the avocado should be neither under nor overripe. After the fruit is cut, it should either be rubbed with lemon juice, or the round stone inside must be left in contact with the fruit, as this prevents discolouration. Avocado is most commonly used cut in half as an hors d'oeuvre. It can also be carved into fans or hedgehogs when just ripe. The flesh of this fruit is rich in oil and vitamins, and its rather low water content is compensated by the nutrients it contains.. But all this goodness comes at a price: 100 gm of avocado flesh has 250 calories!

ALLADIN'S LAMP

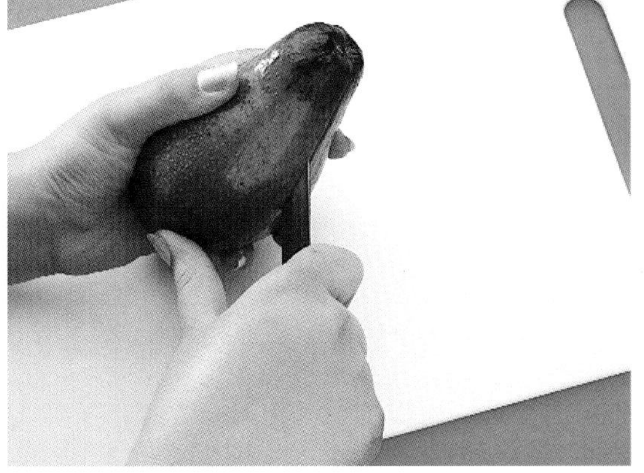

1

1. Using a sharp knife, cut an avocado in half along its length, cutting it up to the stone on all sides.

2. Firmly twist the two sections thus marked in opposite directions and pull them apart. Remove the stone. Apply lemon juice.

2

3

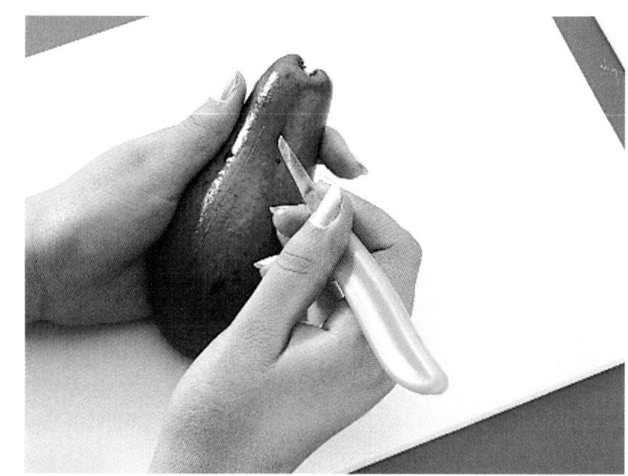

3. Take one half of the avocado and hold the fruit skin side up. With a small knife, starting 1″ away from the narrow end, make two parallel cuts, 1/2″ apart, towards the other end. Stop 1″ short of the broad end.

4. At the narrow end, join the cuts by making a small cut. Then, with the help of the knife, peel away this strip up to the cut point on the opposite side.

5. Turn the avocado over and bring the strip over the broad edge. Fix in place with a toothpick forming the handle.

4

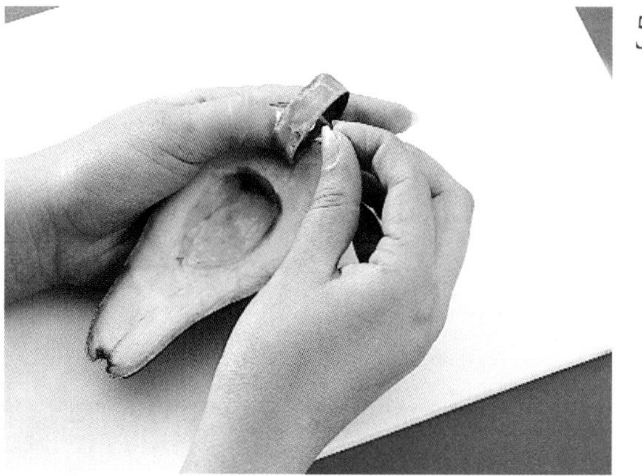

5

6. Fill the stone cavity with vinaigrette dressing, and serve as an elegent hors d'oeuvre.

6

✻ VINAIGRETTE

Ingredients

- 1/2 cup olive oil
- 2 tbsp vinegar
- 1 or 2 tsp powdered sugar
- 1/4 tsp black pepper
- 1/4 tsp mustard
- 1/2 tsp salt

Method

1. Pour the olive oil into a bottle with a screw lid. Add all the ingredients. Screw on the lid and shake the bottle vigorously before using it.
2. If desired, you can add finely chopped gherkins, chives, parsley or any other herbs of your choice. In this picture, paprika flakes have been used to give a hint of colour.

Kiwi

Resembling a dull, furry brown ball, the kiwi is a spectacular fruit when peeled and sliced. It has a green flesh with a starburst of tiny black edible seeds. Slices of kiwi used on desserts or salads give them an exotic appearance.

The kiwi is the fruit of the *actinidia sinesis*, a creeper of Chinese origin, also at times called the Chinese gooseberry. It has in recent years become popular all over the world, and is cultivated on an extremely large scale in New Zealand and California today. Apart from its attractive appearance, the kiwi ranks as one of the most nutritive fruits in the world. One kiwi contains as much vitamin C as several lemons; it is also rich in iron and calcium. The flesh of the ripe fruit is slightly sour, and it should be consumed quickly, as it tends to become rather acidic and unpleasant in taste when overripe.

❊ KIWI PASSION FLOWER

1. Cut a firm kiwi in half horizontally. With a small knife, make 1/2"-deep cuts around the black seeds.

2. Make a slanting cut all around just inside the skin. This cut should join the first one. You have cut a notch all around the black seeds.

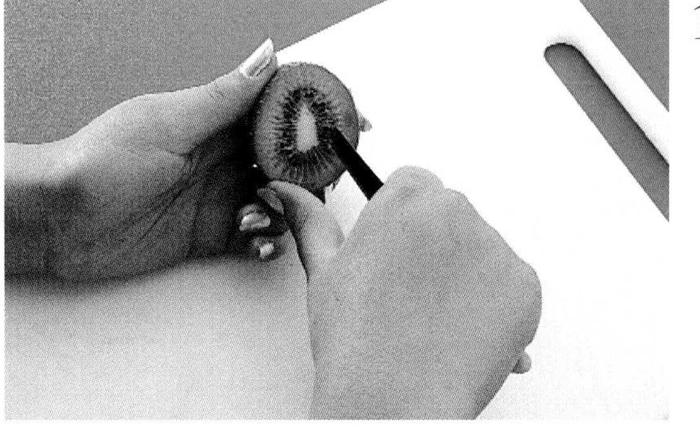

1

2 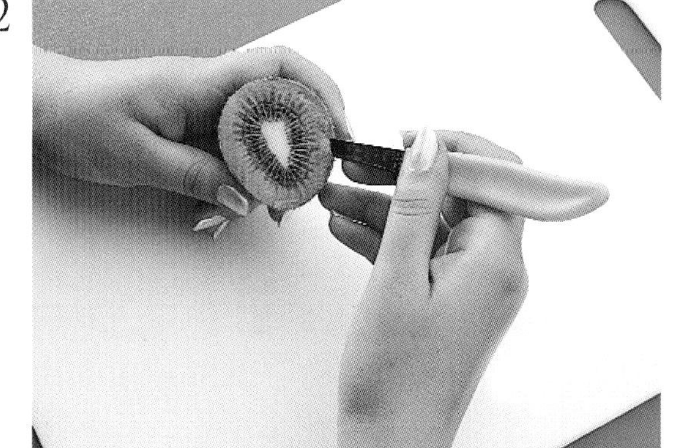

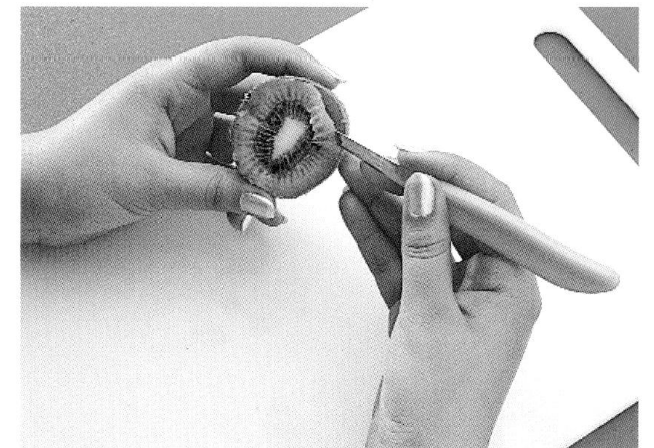 3

4 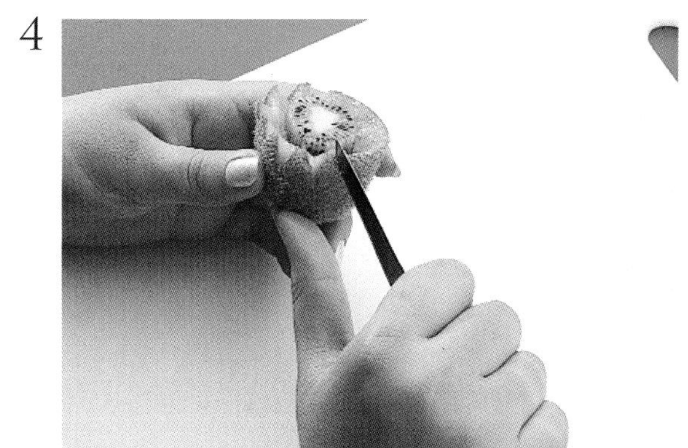

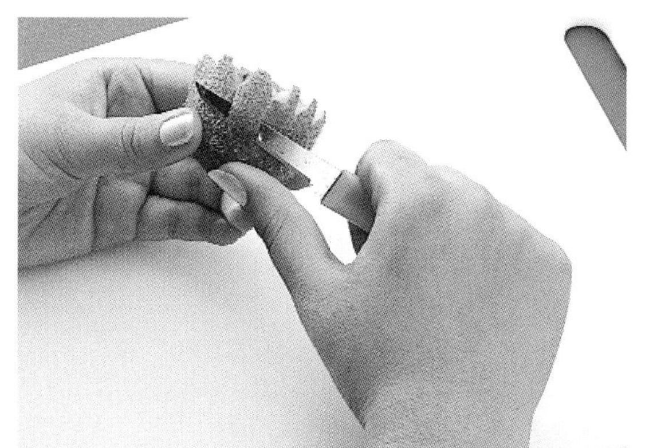 5

3. Remove the flesh from this notch and discard it.

4. Mark the skin side of the kiwi into 12 sections and make v-shaped cuts on these marks. Make vertical cuts down to the base of the fruit (only in the skin), starting from the base of each 'v', and stopping 1/2" away from the base of the fruit.

5. Cut away the skin with a small knife, between two vertical cuts, down to the base of the cuts. You have formed the

6

7

first outer petal. Continue doing this all around the fruit.

6. Neaten the v-shaped grooves to a uniform notched shape. This forms the inner ring of petals.

7. Place the kiwi where desired. Open out the petals to make a complete passion flower.

8

❊ KIWI AND LIME CHEESECAKE

Serves: 8

Ingredients

For the base:

150 gm Marie biscuits
1 tbsp powdered sugar
75 gm butter

For the cheesecake:

1 tbsp cornflour
1 cup milk
4 tsp gelatine, soaked in 4 tbsp water
2 cups curd cheese
3/4 cup sugar
1/4 cup lemon juice
2 ripe mashed kiwis
2 cups whipped cream

For the garnish:

some whipped cream
1 kiwi flower and some kiwi twists (shown on facing page – inset)

Method

1. For the base, crush the biscuits with a rolling pin. Add the powdered sugar and rub in the softened butter. Put this mixture into a loose-bottomed 8″-diameter cake tin and press down firmly. Leave, lightly covered, in a freezer till required.
2. For the cheesecake, mix the cornflour with a little milk in a saucepan. Add the remaining milk and cook over a gentle heat, stirring all the time till the milk is thickened. Remove from heat and keep aside to cool. Meanwhile, melt the gelatine over hot water.
3. In a large bowl or food processor, cream the curd cheese till smooth. Add the thickened milk, sugar, lemon juice and kiwis, and mix well. Now add the cream and gelatine.
4. Pour this mixture over the prepared biscuit base, cover, and keep it in the freezer to set for about four hours.
5. When set, remove from the tin on to a serving platter. Garnish with whipped cream, kiwi flower and twists. Chill till required.

Melon

The fruit of a creeper which grows in hot climates, melons are of two main types: the musk melon and the watermelon. Both grow on sandy riverbeds when the heat of summer sets in. Musk melons are of several varieties, of which honeydew is one of the most popular.

Melons are of different sizes, with watermelons being the biggest, and the colour of their flesh ranges from the palest cream to yellow, peach, orange, pink, and a deep red in the case of watermelons.

Though they are not packed with nutrients, melons are ideal summer fruits, as their copious water content makes them very refreshing on a hot day. Those which are bland and lacking in flavour can be served with lemon juice and sugar.

❊ MELON BASKET

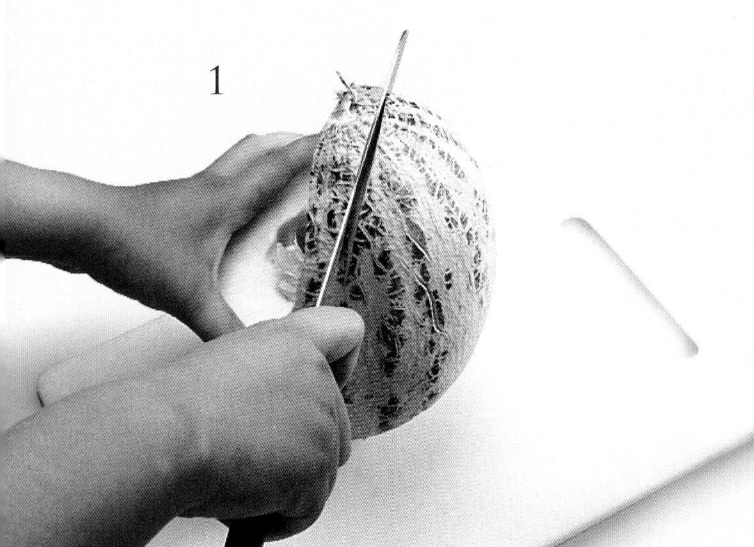

1. Take a large melon. Slice off a small piece from the bottom to create a steady base. Place the melon on a flat surface. Now make a cut from the top, starting about 3/4" away from the centre, cutting downwards towards the base. Cut only half way down. On the same side, make a cut

2

3

sideways from the middle towards the downwards cut, so that they meet. Remove this piece. Repeat this procedure on the other side. It should now look like a basket with a handle. Trim wherever needed to give it a perfect shape.

2. Scoop out the seeds.

3. Using a melon baller, scoop out balls from the two pieces of melon and from the wedge of watermelon.

4. If desired, scoop out balls from the 'basket' as well.

❋ STUFFED MELON BASKET

Serves: 4-6

Ingredients

1 melon, large
a wedge of watermelon
any other fruit (optional)
2 tbsp lemon juice
2 tbsp castor sugar
1 tsp ginger powder
1/2 tsp black pepper, crushed
1 tsp mint, finely chopped (optional)
1 or 2 slices of carambola
a few cherries and mint leaves

Method

1. Make a melon basket as instructed on pp. 24 and 25.
2. In a bowl, combine the melon and the watermelon balls with any other fruits of your choice. Sprinkle lemon juice, sugar, ginger powder, pepper and mint. Toss well and pile into the melon basket.
3. Decorate with carambola slices, cherries and mint leaves, and keep it in a cool place till it is served.

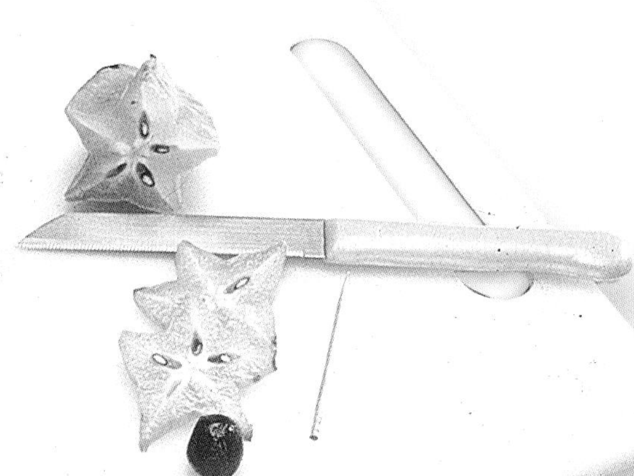

Orange

A sun-kissed fruit that grows in many parts of the world, oranges are very popular and well known for their nutritive value and thirst-quenching properties. They come in many sizes and hues – from gold to deepest orange; and their flavour ranges from extremely tart to very sweet. California, Florida, Africa, South America and some Mediterranean countries are the largest producers of these luscious and juicy fruits.

Oranges are a rich source of vitamin C and are low in calories. They make a refreshing dessert in summer, and can be made into juice, marmalade and salads. Orange rind has a wonderful tangy zest (because it contains citrus oil) and is used as a flavouring.

❊ ORANGE SUNBURST

An orange or any other citrus fruit with a loose skin is suitable for this.

1. Take an orange that is firm and has a good skin colour.

2. With a sharp knife, cut the skin into eight sections. Start at the top centre

1

2

3

and leave about 3/4″ uncut at the base of each section.

3. Gently pull out the sections of the skin so that they open out like a flower. Ensure that the orange segments remain intact.

4. Holding each section of the skin flat on the chopping board, make petal-shaped cuts inside each section, again leaving about 3/4″ uncut. You have cut a petal within a petal.

5. Fold the outer sections of the peel upwards and tuck them under the orange. The smaller petals will curl up, giving a sunburst effect.

4

5

6. This is a simple and attractive way to serve an orange as a dessert. Peal it and place a couple of mint leaves on top of it. Alternately, brush the top with lemon juice, sprinkle with castor sugar, and then place the mint leaves on top.

6

~

❊ ORANGE RIND STRIPS

1. Mark the entire skin of an orange in eight sections and peel them off. Lay a section of the skin flat on a chopping board, pith side up. Holding it flat firmly with one hand, start cutting through between the white portion and the coloured skin, using a sharp or small serrated knife.

2. Continue this process, moving the knife in a sawing motion, till all the white portion is removed. Cut the remaining coloured rind in very thin and long strips with a knife or scissors.

1

2

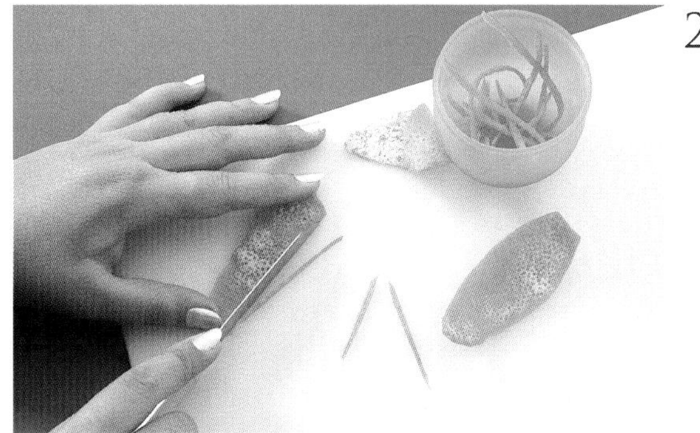

3. In a small bowl or bottle, add the juice of two or three limes and about 1/4 cup sugar to the rinds. Allow it to steep for a few hours, or a couple of days. These are delicious tossed into a light green salad, or as a garnish for a dessert.

~

1

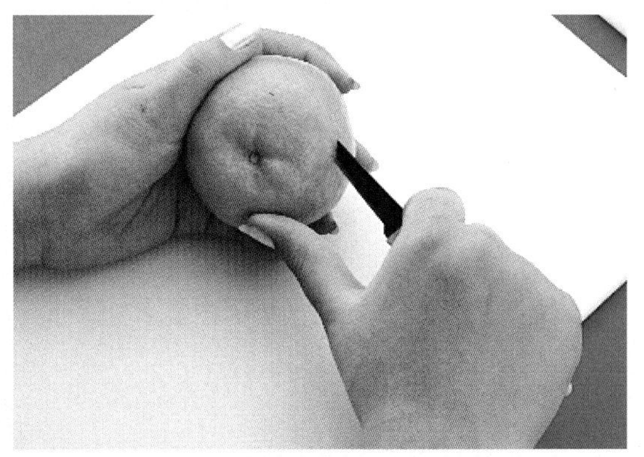

2

❊ ORANGE SORBET CUPS

Serves: 4

Ingredients

2 cups orange juice and pulp
1 cup sugar
1 cup water
4 tbsp lemon juice
1/2 cup double cream
1 egg white
4 hollowed-out orange skins with 'lids', mint leaves and cherries as garnish

Method

1. To make orange cups, cut 1" from the stem end horizontally. Keep aside the cutaway piece for the lid.

2. Scoop out the segments from the cup and lid with a spoon. Keep aside.
3. Boil the sugar and water in a pan. Lower the heat and let it simmer for about 10 minutes. Remove the syrup from the heat and skim off any froth or matter that comes to the surface. Allow it to cool.
4. Add the lemon and orange juice to the syrup and mix well. Then place it in a freezer till it is almost set. This process will take at least three to four hours.
5. Whip the double cream and the egg white separately.
6. Remove the frozen juice from the freezer, and break it up into pieces with a fork. Fold in the cream and then the whipped egg white. Freeze it till it is quite set, for another three to four hours.
7. Before serving, remove the sorbet from the freezer, and fill up the orange skins with it, piling it up generously right to the top. Place the lid on it and secure with a toothpick on which you have impaled a cherry and a mint leaf.
8. To make the sorbet look exotic, place extra orange skins, cut sunburst fashion, below each sorbet cup.

Papaya

The papaya is the fruit of a very quick-growing tropical tree which is native to warm tropical countries. Its flesh ranges in colour from golden yellow to a deep reddish orange, and its size from 6″ to just over a foot in length. The ripe fruit is very sweet and tastes wonderful with a dash of lemon juice. Inside the fleshy fruit are small black seeds, each in a membranous sack of its own. These are the only inedible portion of the entire papaya tree, for besides the fruit, the leaves and trunk of the tree abound in an enzyme called papain, which is extremely efficacious – it aids digestion, heals wounds, and is used for other medicinal purposes. Unripe papaya is a wonderful meat tenderiser. Ripe papaya is a good source of vitamin A, as it is rich in carotene. It also contains vitamin C in abundance. Papaya can easily be carved into boat, bowl and lantern shapes.

PAPAYA LANTERN

1. Peel a firm ripe papaya. Make a simple template with a paper folded in eighths. Place the template on the papaya where desired and cut out the design through it with a small, sharp knife. Remember that the papaya will be used with the stem portion as the base.

1

1

2

3

4

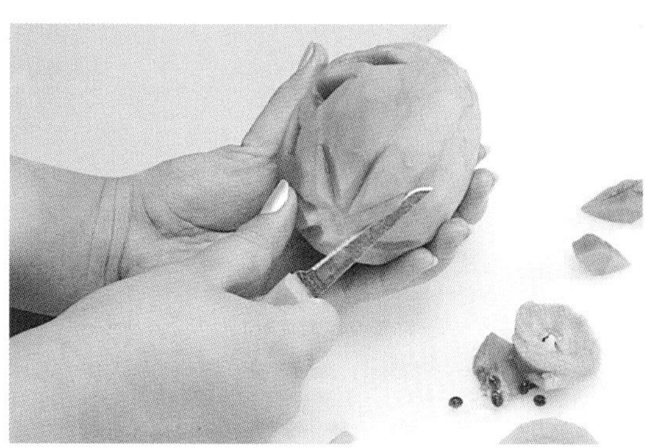

2. Cut off the stem end below the cut out pattern to form a base. The seed cavity should be exposed.

3. Scoop out all the seeds through the opening with a teaspoon.

4. Make a serrated pattern on the top of the papaya.

5. Decorate with a cherry on top. Light a small candle and put it on a plate. Place the papaya over it. The light will shine through with a beautiful orange glow.

Note: This is an eye-catching decoration for a buffet table.

Peach

The peach grew wild in China thousands of years ago, and from there it spread to other parts of the world. Now it grows wherever there is plenty of sunshine. Peaches contain an appreciable amount of vitamin C, and some minerals and carotene. A ripe, luscious peach is delicious, whether it is eaten fresh, had as a juice, or made into jam.

Peaches are of two main types: free stone and cling stone. In the former, the stone is separated easily from the flesh, but in the latter it is hard to remove. This fruit can vary in size from the size of a walnut to that of an apple. The colour of some varieties is a pale green with a pink blush, and others veer to golden orange with an almost maroonish bloom.

PEACH LOTUS

1. Cut 1″ off the lower end of a free-stone peach. Mark lightly with eight equidistant notches.

1

2. Using a small knife, cut out eight 'v' shapes, using the notches as a guide. The peach will have eight

2

3

4

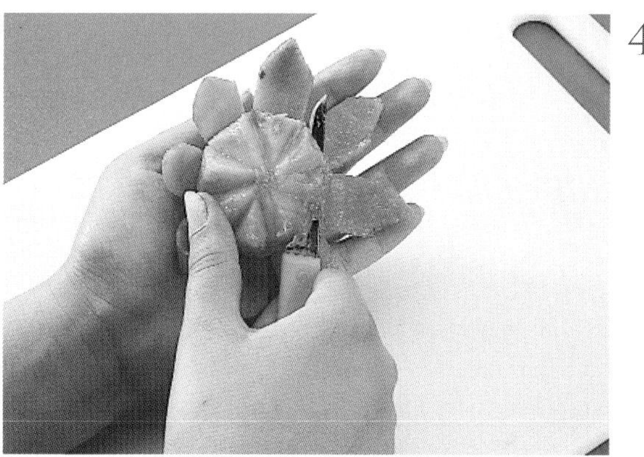

zigzag indentations on the cut end. Now make vertical cuts (on the skin), from the base of each notch towards the stem end, stopping 3/4″ away from the ends, forming eight petals.

3. Cut out petals, to the base of the cuts.

4. Neaten the notches on the flesh, and remove the stone carefully.

5. Fill the cavity with strawberry jam. Place the peach on a serving plate, and pipe a swirl of cream on the side. Serve this as a simple dessert.

Note: For a memorable dessert, fill each peach lotus with some peach cream. (Serve the remaining peach cream separately.) To make peach cream, mix a cup of peach pulp with sugar to taste, and fold it into a cup of whipped cream.

5

Pear

Pears are fleshy fruits that grow in the temperate region. There are several varieties of this fruit, which range in texture from hard to soft, with varying juice content. They ripen and spoil quickly, but are so good to eat, that the little extra effort required to preserve them, by brushing them with lemon juice, is well worth it. All the different varieties of pears have the same basic qualities: a delightfully delicate flavour and taste that lingers in the mouth.

❋ PEAR CUPS

1

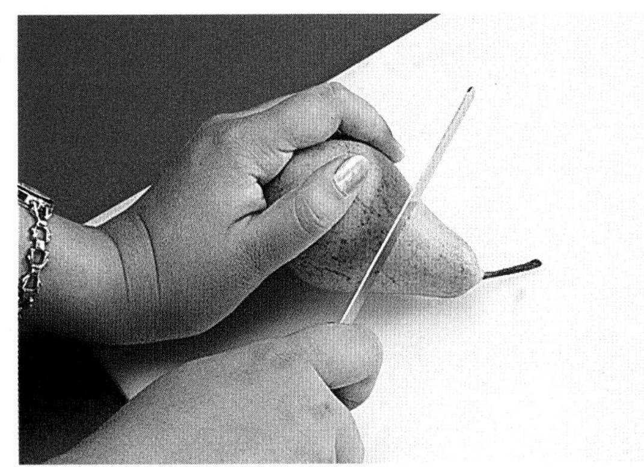

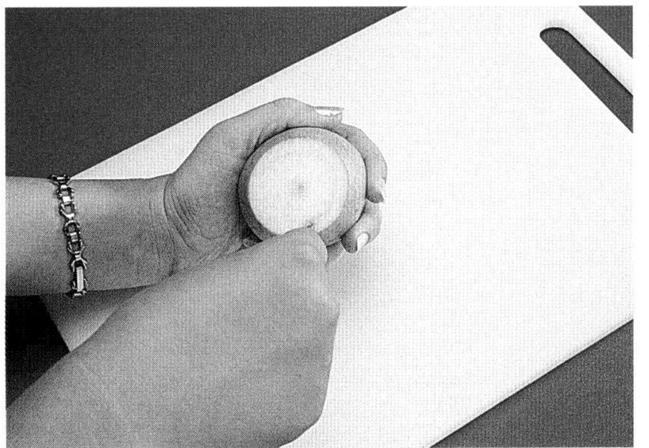

2

1. Take a firm and almost ripe pear with a broad base. Slice off one-third from the top.

2. Run a small, sharp knife all around inside the top edge of the fruit to mark a groove measuring about 1/4″- 1/2″.

3 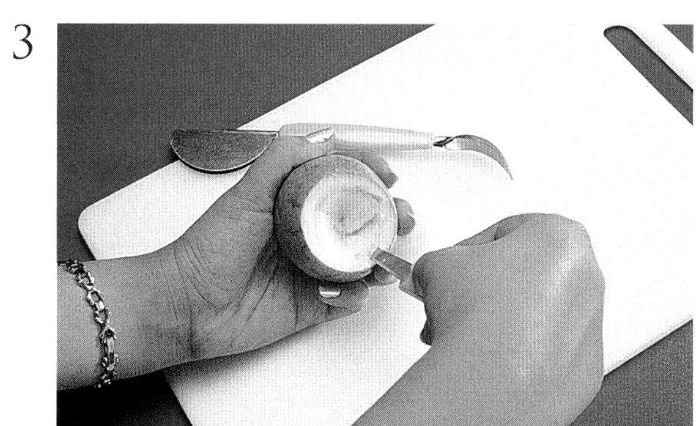

4 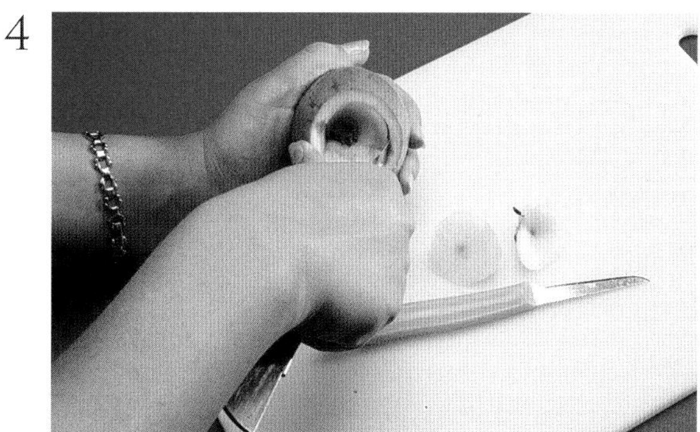

5 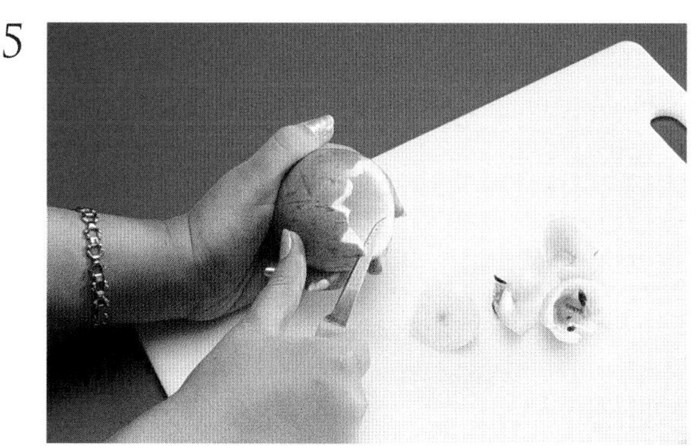

3. Hold the pear firmly in your left hand, in the hollow of your palm. With a curved grapefruit knife, cut through it slowly in a circular motion, manipulating the knife blade carefully till you reach the base of the pear.

4. Now scoop out and clean the inner portion thoroughly with the help of a teaspoon. Brush the inside of the pear with lemon juice and keep it aside till required.

5. Your pear cup is now ready. (You can peel the skin, if you like, just before serving it.) This can be used either as a fruit bowl to serve cherries and other small fruits, or to garnish a spiced pear salad.

❊ COLD SPICED PEARS

Serves: 4

Ingredients

4 firm ripe pears
1 cup cabbage, finely shredded
1/2 cup onion greens, chopped
1/2 cup canned cherries, drained
white vinegar (for marination)
1 tsp fresh pepper, coarsely ground
1 tsp paprika flakes

For the dressing:

2 tbsp lemon juice
2 tbsp powdered sugar
1 tbsp oil
salt to tast
extra lemon juice, to brush on pears

Method

1. Mix the cherries with vinegar and put them into a cup. Keep them aside for at least half an hour.
2. Make the pear cups, as shown earlier. Reserve the pieces which have been taken out, to add to the filling. Peel the pears and brush them with lemon juice.
3. Mix together the shredded cabbage, pieces of pear, onion greens, pepper and paprika.
4. Mix all the ingredients for the dressing in a jar and shake vigorously. Pour this over the cabbage mixture and mix well.
5. Fill all the cups with this mixture, and press down firmly.
6. Drain the cherries and arrange them on top of the cups.

(This is a unique and refreshing hors d' oeuvre to serve on a warm day.)

Mango

The mango is a popular tropical fruit, known in some countries as the king of fruits. Its unique flavour is relished by almost everyone who has ever tasted it. There are several varieties of this luscious fruit. Mango skin is deep green in colour, and its flesh extremely sour when unripe – it is used to make salads, chutneys, jellies and pickles. What is really amazing is how such a sour fruit can become so sweet and delicious when ripe!

❊ MANGO HEDGEHOGS

1

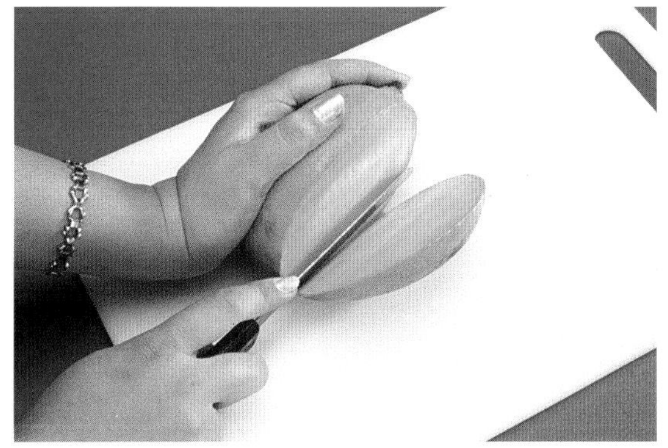

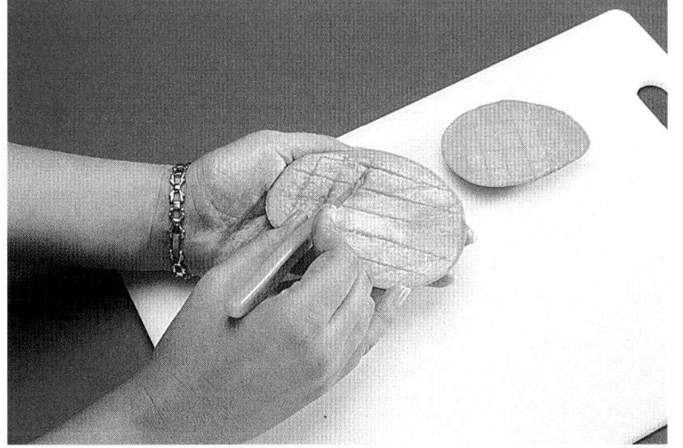

2

1. Take a ripe, firm mango – avoid using the fibrous variety. Slice off two pieces from either side of the stone. Cut parallel lines, about 1/2"-3/4" apart, along the length of the mango slice.

2. Cut parallel lines at right angles to these, the same distance apart. You must go right down to the skin, but be extremely careful that you do not cut through it.

3. Hold the slice firmly, and with the tips of your fingers, push it out from the back, carefully, applying pressure on the thickest part. The slice will open out to resemble a hedgehog, and will retain this shape. Use this as a garnish to decorate fruit desserts.

❊ INLAID MANGO SLICES

1. Cut two slices from both sides of a mango. (Be careful that you do not use a fibrous fruit.) For the inlay, use a thickly cut strip of apple peal. Cut three or four small flowers from the apple peel, using a flower cutter.

2

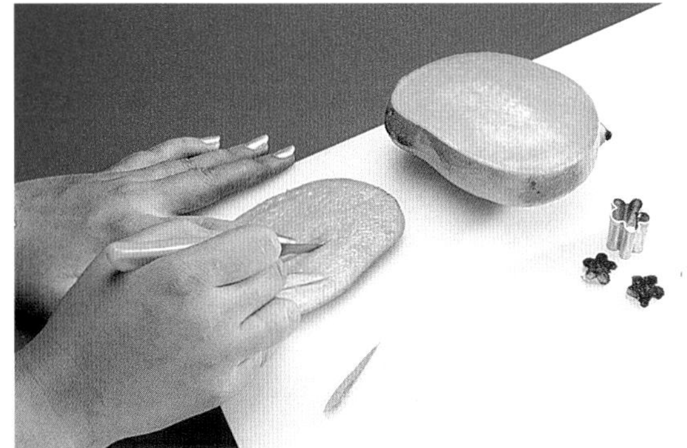

3

2. Arrange the flowers on the mango slice, in order to see how they will look when they are placed there. Then scoop out the pulp from the fruit with a melon baller, to create grooves for the flowers to be inserted. The depth of each groove should be sufficient to accommodate a flower.

3. Now place thin strips of green lime rind below the flowers, to make stems and leaves. Cut grooves with a knife to fit these in. Press in the flowers and leaves.

4. Chill these inlaid slices and use them as garnishing for mango desserts.

4

✻ MANGO SURPRISE

Serves: 4

Ingredients

4 firm ripe mangoes
1 cup cream cheese
4 tbsp castor sugar
1 tbsp lemon juice
a few small flower cutouts
a few small leaf cutouts

For the garnish:
whipped cream for decoration
small mango balls

Method

1. Cut away two slices from both sides of the mangoes, cutting as close to the stone as possible. Flatten the sides of the slices by cutting smaller slices from them.You now have four slices from each mango – two large and two small. Remove the pulp from the small slices and discard the peel.
2. Cut out oval rings from the insides of four of the slices – they should be about 1/2″ thick. Place them on individual serving dishes.
3. Inlay flowers and leaves, as shown earlier, on the remaining four slices of mangoes.
4. Mash the pulp you have removed from the rings, and mix it with the pulp from the small slices. Then mix together the pulp, cream cheese, sugar and lemon juice. Check for taste, and adjust it according to the tartness of the fruit.
5. Fill the oval mango rings with this mixture – if there is any left over, it can be formed into fancy shapes and arranged on the sides of the dish. Smoothen the top of the filling and carefully arrange the inlaid mango slices on it.
6. Pipe rosettes of whipped cream on the sides of the serving dish. Top them with small mango balls.

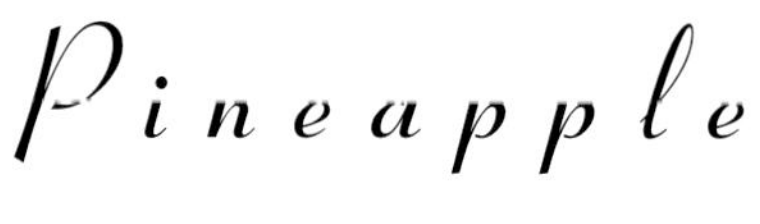

Pineapple

Pineapples grow on shrubs which thrive in humid, tropical climatic conditions. They originated in tropical America and were taken all over the world by sailors and traders. The plant, *ananas comosus*, is now widely grown in all tropical countries. The fruit is extensively canned and is available almost everywhere.

This attractive fruit is borne on a strong stem which emerges from the centre of a cluster of stiff leaves. It is oval in shape (with a plume of leaves on top); green and yellow in colour; and the surface of the skin is hard and knobbly, giving the fruit an exotic look. The skin itself is thick and rough, with prickly scales on the knobs.

Pineapples should be eaten when their base changes from green to yellow. Since the skin is tough and thick, only about 60 per cent of the fruit is edible. It is rich in vitamins B1 and C. Fresh pineapple juice contains an enzyme which is good for digestion, and also acts as a diuretic. However, even if the fruit is slightly overripe, it is acidic and inedible.

Though pineapples are used a lot in salads and desserts, care must be taken not to include it in dishes that have to be set using gelatine – the enzyme present in the fruit does not allow gelatine to set.

1

2

❊ PINEAPPLE BOWL

1. Take a firm, ripe pineapple with a healthy plume of leaves. Using a chef's knife, carefully cut the fruit in two perfect halves.

2. With a small, sharp knife, cut deeply all around inside the pineapple, 3/4″ away from the skin. Then make a straight incision in the middle of the fruit, starting from the leaves to the opposite side, right down to 1/2″ away from the skin.

3

3. Using a grape-fruit knife, cut and ease away half the flesh. Then remove the second half of the fruit. Your bowl in ready to fill.

1

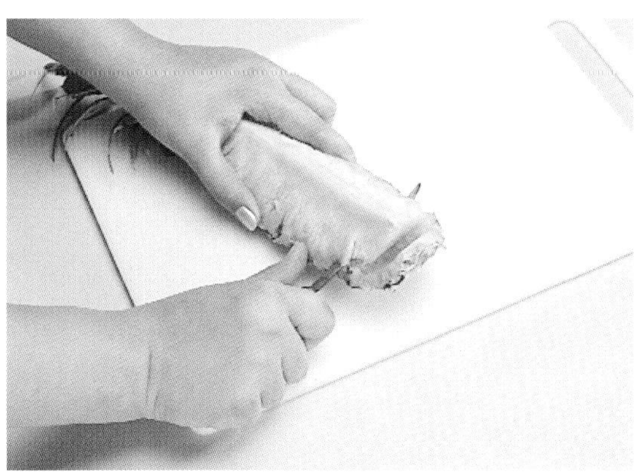

2

❊ PINEAPPLE BOAT

1. Cut a pineapple in half, cutting through the plumes as well. Now divide these two parts in half again.

2. Using a grapefruit knife, cut away the flesh, 3/4″ away from the skin. Cut the pineapple flesh in 3/4″ slices.

3. Place these slices back in the shell, arranging them in a zigzag fashion. Decorate with some cherries on both sides, and two plastic cocktail picks on one side. Make a sail with a thin slice of watermelon on a satay stick, and garnish with a cherry and a twist of lemon rind.

3

❊ PINEAPPLE SALAD

Serves: 4

Ingredients

- 1/2 pineapple, cut horizontally, with the leaves intact
- 1 apple, large and thickly peeled
- 1 peach, large, or a medium-sized mango, peeled and diced
- 1/2 green capsicum, finely diced
- 1 tbsp parsley or mint, chopped

For the dressing:

- 2 tbsp oil
- 2 tbsp lemon juice
- 2 tbsp sugar
- 1/4 tsp garlic, ground
- salt and pepper to taste
- a few paprika flakes

For the garnish:

- 3 or 4 apple-peel flowers
- a slice of carombola and a cherry

Method

1. Take out the flesh of the pineapple, as for the pineapple bowl. Cut away the hard inner core, and dice the fruit, reserving any juice. This can be added to the dressing. Keep the hollowed-out shell to serve the salad.
2. Make some tiny daisies from apple peel. They will be used as decoration. Cut the apple into fine juliennes.
3. Mix the apple juliennes, the peach or mango, capsicum, and parsley or mint together, and keep in a cool place.
4. For the dressing, mix all the ingredients in a screw-topped bottle.
5. To serve, shake the bottle, and pour the dressing over the salad. Mix well, pile the mixture into the pineapple shell, and garnish with apple daisies, carombola and cherries.

Strawberry

Luscious, ripe, red strawberries are delightful to eat and beautiful to behold. Their rich taste and flavour has been compared to ambrosia!

Originally strawberries grew in the shade of pines on the foothills – they still grow wild. Today, due to modern technological and agricultural advancement, fresh strawberries are found in parts of the world where they were only dreamt of earlier. Nowadays, the strawberries in demand are large, perfectly shaped and deep red, unlike their wild predecessor. This emphasis on appearance has resulted in loss of flavour, which is diminished by hybridisation. Strawberries are a rich source of vitamin C.

Because they are soft, delicate and small in size, these fruits are difficult to carve, except in the most simple forms. They can, however, be dipped in fondant or melted chocolate and used as edible decoration on desserts.

❊ STRAWBERRY FANS AND SLICES

1. Take a firm, red strawberry and cut it into several slices. Start at the pointed end, and cut towards the stem end, not slicing it right through.
2. With thumb and fingers, prise open the strawberry slices in a fan-like fashion. Use them as decoration on desserts.

1

2

3

Slices of strawberry can be formed into simple flower shapes.

With these variables, you can fabricate simple, eye-catching flowers.

3. Make a simple flower with five strawberry slices. Use mint leaves for the stem and leaves. You can use flat inner slices, or curved slices from the sides – the slices can be used with the pointed ends as outer or inner edges.

4. To make a poinsettia, place eight or ten slices in a circle. Arrange another row of slices inside this circle. Then fill up the centre with two or three small slices. You can make the poinsettia with two or three rows of slices.

STRAWBERRY POINSETTIA PIE

Serves: 6

Ingredients

For the biscuit crust:

150 gm Marie biscuits
1 tbsp sugar, powdered
75 gm unsalted butter

For the filling:

1 strawberry jelly packet
1 cup water
3/4 cup curd cheese
1/2 cup cream
1 tbsp lemon juice
4 tbsp sugar
1 cup strawberries, puréed
3/4 cup thick pouring cream
a few strawberry slices
a little green-coloured whipped cream

Method

1. For the biscuit base, crush the biscuits finely with a rolling pin and keep in a bowl. Add the sugar and unsalted butter and mix well. Take some mixture in your hand and press it in your fist. If it retains a ball shape, it is of the right consistency. If it crumbles, add some more unsalted butter.
2. Put this mixture in an 8″ loose-bottomed pie tin, and press down firmly with a flat-bottomed bowl. Press it firmly into the sides as well. Cover lightly and keep it in the freezer to set.
3. For the filling, mix the jelly crystals with the water in a saucepan, and leave it aside for a minute. Then melt it over hot water. Stir well till all the crystals dissolve. Remove and keep aside.
4. Mix together the curd cheese and cream. Add the lemon juice, sugar and strawberry purée. Stir this into the cooled jelly and pour the mixture into the prepared pie shell. Cover lightly and freeze for two to three hours.
5. Remove from the freezer and pour the cream over the filling. Keep it in the refrigerator until you want to serve it. Place the pie on a serving platter. Decorate it with strawberry slices arranged like a poinsettia, and pipe stems and leaves with green cream.

Watermelon

There are differing opinions regarding where watermelons first grew. While some people believe it originated in north Africa, others think that India can claim that honour. They need hot and dry climatic conditions and grow well on sandy river banks. The creepers are 6-10 feet in length, and each plant bears several fruits, each of which can weigh up to 40 pounds. The fruit is green on the outside, with varying shades of pink, orange and red on the inside, and its shape varies from a perfect round to a flattish oval. Watermelons are a good source of vitamins and are also a diuretic.

❊ WATERMELON DAHLIA

A spectacular centrepiece for a fruit arrangement or platter

1. With a chef's knife, slice a small watermelon in half horizontally. (You will require only half a fruit to make a dahlia.) Using a medium-sized sharp knife, cut away the green skin. Leave at least 1/4" of the white flesh all around the watermelon. This will give a beautiful shaded effect to the dahlia petals finally, when they have been carved.

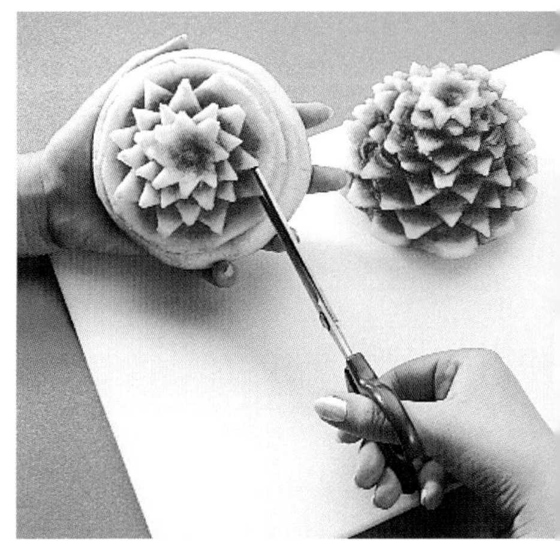

2. Using a small, sharp knife, mark a small groove right at the top centre of the watermelon – this will be the central portion of the dahlia. Then make a 3/4"-deep cut, in a circle, 3/4" away from the groove. This cut should be at an inward angle of 45° – try to keep this angle constant. This means that the tip of the knife should be angled towards the central groove.

3. Now make a parallel cut, about 1/4" away from the first cut, all around. The tip of the knife should meet the base of the first cut. This means that you are cutting out a v-shaped notch in a circle. Remove the flesh of the notch. You now have a circular v-shaped groove all around the central groove.

4. Repeat steps 2 and 3, starting 3/4" away from the previous groove, all the way down to the base of the watermelon. For the dahlia to be a success, it is important that the angle of all the grooves is almost the same.

5. Now, with the scissors, cut out v-shaped petals about 3/4" wide, all around the top of the watermelon, cutting the flesh that lies between the two uppermost grooves.

6 Proceed like this downwards towards the base, cutting out circles of petals. (The petals of each circle should be between the petals of the previous row.)

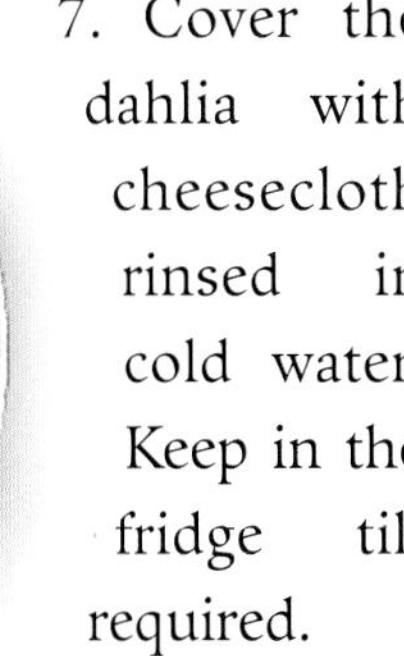

7. Cover the dahlia with cheesecloth rinsed in cold water. Keep in the fridge till required.

1

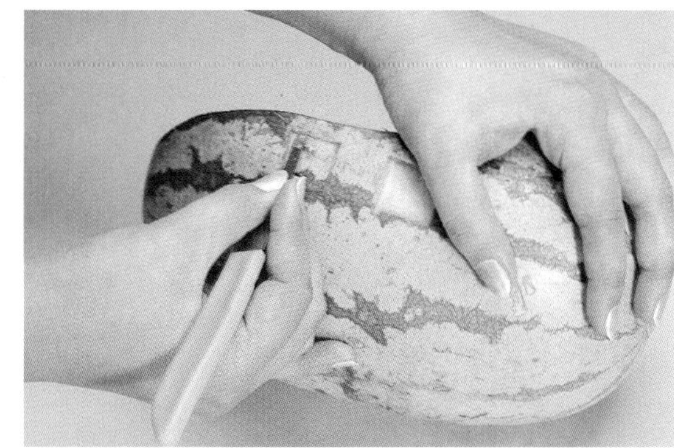

5

❊ WATERMELON SHIP

1. Make one side along the length of a watermelon a flat base by cutting off a 1″-thick slice from the fruit. Place this on a plain and smooth surface. Ensure that the watermelon is lying straight and not tilting to either side.

2. Starting from the stem end, carefully slice the watermelon in half horizontally, about two-thirds of the way, right through the other end. The cut surface should be as flat and even as possible.

3. Now start slicing from the top of the fruit, downwards, right down to the horizontal cut. Remove the piece of fruit you have cut out and keep it aside. The protruding one-third portion of the uncut watermelon will be used to form the rear cabin of the watermelon ship.

4. Flatten the top of the rear cabin by cutting off a 1″-thick slice horizontally from the top.

5. Etch out 1″ squares on the watermelon rind, skin deep, with the tip of a sharp knife, on both sides of the ship – these will form the portholes.

6

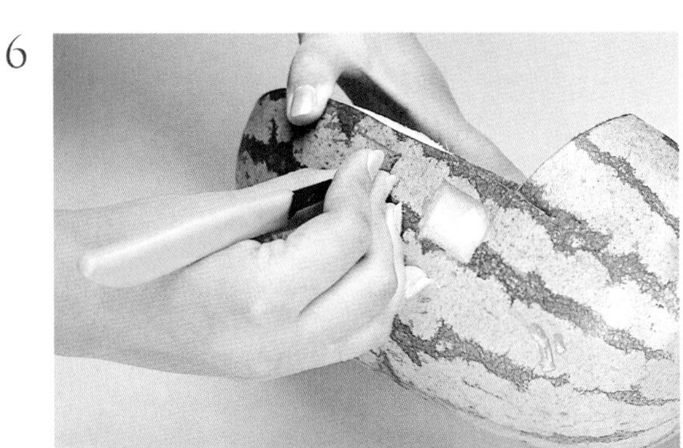

7

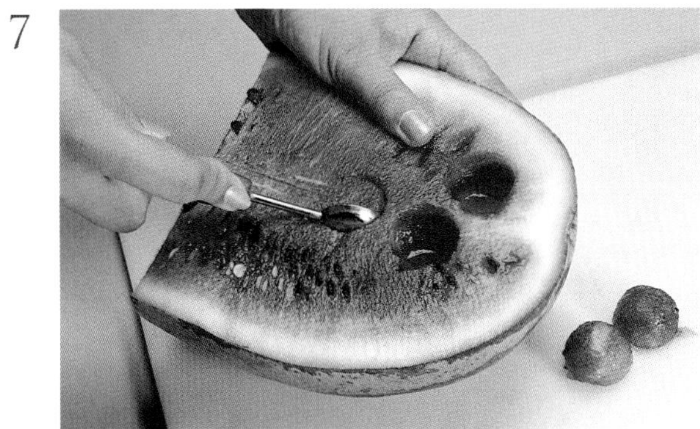

8

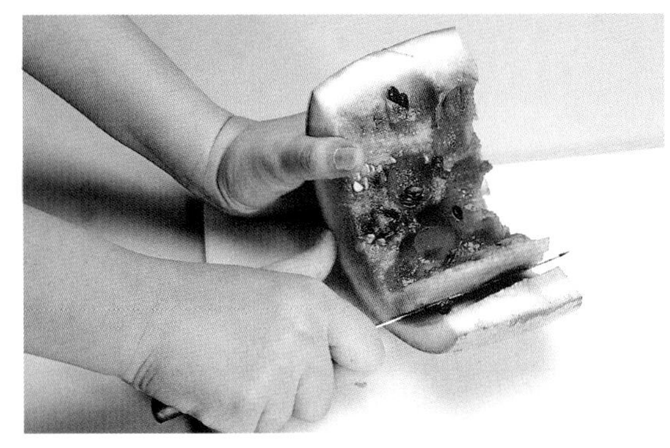

6. Holding the knife almost flat, remove the rind from inside the squares.

7. With a 1″ melon baller, cut away as many balls from the reserved piece of watermelon as possible.

8. Cut the rind into three pieces along the width and remove the remaining flesh.

9. Cut the biggest piece of rind into three equal sections and remove the peel from all the pieces.

10. Remove any flesh with a cleaver, and cut the remaining two pieces of the rind – the bigger piece should be cut into two triangles and one rectangle. Trim and shape the third tapering piece into a triangle. You have seven pieces left to form the sails.

11. Skewer these pieces on satay sticks to make them look like the sails of a

9

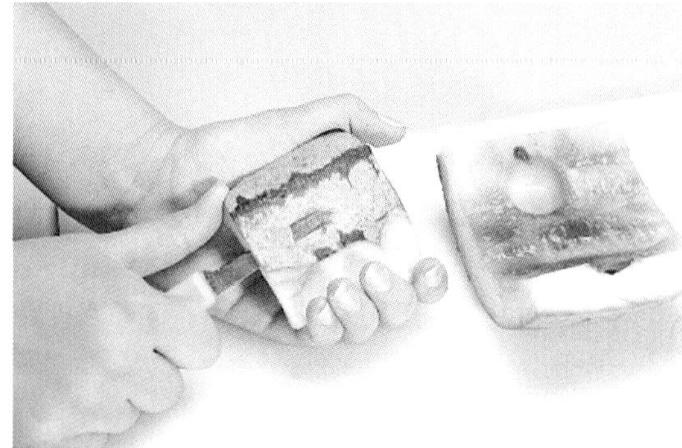

10

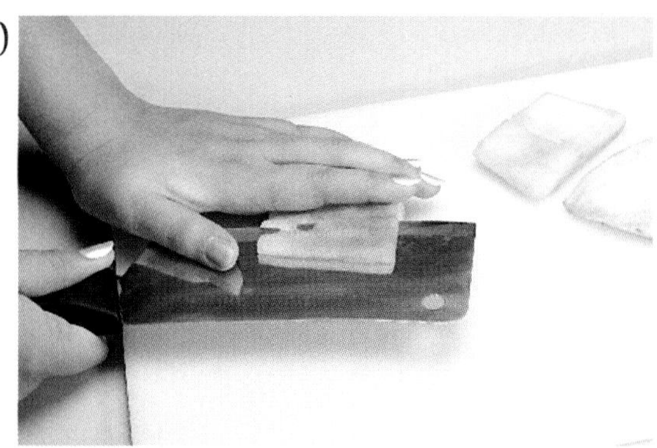

11

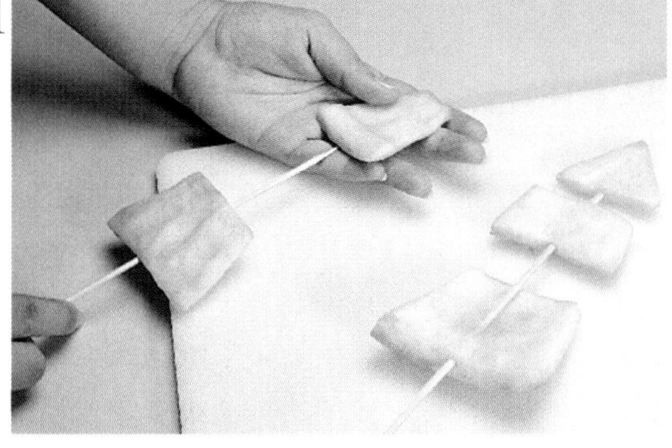

ship. Fix the sails on the centre of the ship and some of the watermelon balls all around the top deck, on the edges. Then place the remaining balls all over the deck.

12. Arrange the wooden cocktail skewers on both sides of the ship, to resemble oars.

Etch out three windows on the rind at the back of the cabin. Also carve a name, if desired.

13. Cover the ship with a cheesecloth which has been soaked in cold water and wrung out. Keep in a cool place till required.

12

Vegetables

Cabbage

Cabbages have been cultivated since early times, especially in central Europe. They were an important part of the staple diet of man since the days he lived on roots and herbs. Even today, they are eaten all over the world, largely because they are cheap and easily accessible to all.

Cabbages belong to the *brassica oleracia* (mustard) family. The common cabbage, the Savoy, broccoli, red cabbage and the cauliflower, all belong to this family and are popular the world over. Cabbages are of two varieties: the summer and the winter varieties. Therefore, this vegetable is easily available throughout the year.

Uncooked cabbage has a high vitamin content, is very low in calories, and is considered to be a diuretic. It is popular in this form in salads. Cooked cabbage, however, is not very popular, as the subtle flavour of this vegetable is diminished by cooking it. However, the leaves rolled up in bundles, after being filled, and then cooked, make a tasty dish; and the whole cabbage head can also be hollowed out, stuffed with a filling, and steamed.

On the following page, a cabbage head is used as an interesting bowl for a cream dip.

1

2

3

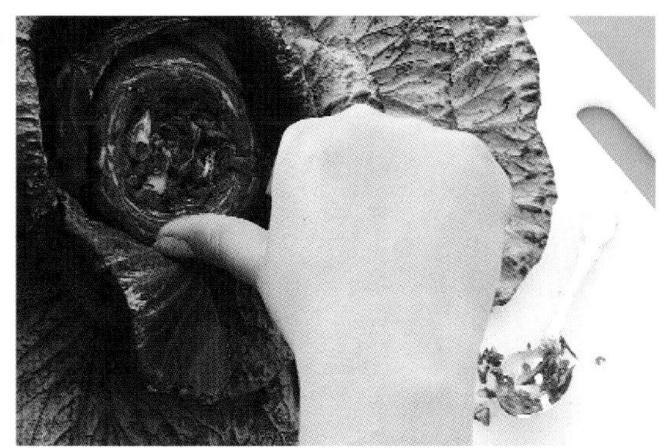

❊ CABBAGE BOWL

For this you require a cabbage with the rough outer leaves intact, though you can carve a bowl out of just the head.

1. Trim any damaged leaves, ensuring there are enough good leaves left to fan out. Cut the stalk to make the cabbage lie flat, and lop off the top of the head.

2. With a small, sharp knife, stab the cabbage at random, and start pulling out the pieces, little by little. Keep doing this till you have literally gouged out the inside of the cabbage head. Start prising out the inner leaves. They should come out easily now.

3. Pull out as many leaves as you think necessary, making sure that there are still enough left to give the sides of the 'bowl' strength.

4. This exotic bowl can be placed on a buffet table and used for a dip, or fill it with a salad of your choice.

❊ CREAM CHEESE BOWL

Ingredients

1 head of red cabbage
500 gm yoghurt
1 cup cream
1 tsp garlic, ground
2 spring onions, finely chopped
1 tbsp parsley, chopped
2 tbsp olive oil
salt and pepper to taste

Method

1. Prepare the cabbage head as shown on the previous page.
2. Place the yoghurt in a clean muslin cloth, and hang it up for about five to six hours, till all the water drains out.
3. In a bowl, add the drained yoghurt, and mix it with a wooden spoon till it is smooth in texture. Pour in the cream, stirring continuously. Add the remaining ingredients and adjust the seasoning according to taste.
4. Keep this mixture covered in a cool place till it is time to serve it. It should be allowed to 'rest' for at least half an hour to let the flavour develop.
5. Before serving, take one or two teaspoons of the mixture, and scrape it against the outer edges of several outer leaves in order to give them a frosted look. Put the remaining mixture into the cabbage bowl and serve melba toast, breadsticks or salted crackers with it.

Innovative Slices and Chunks

All fruits and vegetables can be sliced, and they can also be twisted or carved. Just by arranging the slices in different ways, it is possible to enhance the appearance of a dish.

1. Five or six round or oval slices of white radish or carrot can be impaled on satay sticks to form flowers, and small vegetable balls or round shapes used as centres for the flowers. In the picture, broccoli florets and red radish flowers, looking very real, are arranged on a cabbage base (flattened on one side for stability).
2. Very thin cucumber slices can be overlapped to resemble fish scales. This arrangement looks particularly good as a garnish on poached fish.
3. Slices of apples and lemons can have simple designs carved on their skins, as shown in the picture below. The vivid contrast between the colours of the fruits and vegetables and their skin is highlighted very effectively. It is an innovative way of serving them.
4. Fruits and vegetables can be cut into bite-sized chunks. (Leave the skin on for colour.) Cut the chunks into circles, squares, triangles, rectangles or ovals, about 1/2″ thick, and use them in salads. The bright colours and shapes will greatly enhance their appearance.
5. To achieve a really festive look, etch simple designs on vegetables and fruits. It is not at all difficult, and adds an exotic touch to simple table decorations and salads.

Capsicum

Capsicums, the fruits of the *capsicum annuum* plant, are believed to have originated in South America. The colourful 'bell peppers' also belong to the same family. Capsicums and peppers are either box-like in shape or conical. The one most commonly available is the green pepper, and it is cooked in several ways. The other peppers are red, yellow, orange and black. Peppers are rather expensive, but add so much colour to any dish that they are well worth the money spent on them. Uncooked peppers add pungency and crispness to any salad or dish. They can also be sauteed, baked, roasted and fried, and, with olive oil and garlic, make a delicious tongue- tingling salad.

✻ PEPPER FLOWERS

1

1. Select peppers of different colours. With a small sharp knife, make deep jagged cuts all around, close to the stem end.

2. Gently separate the two halves, being careful not to damage the 'petals'.

3. You will get one flower (seed side) and one cup. Trim away any membranes from both the halves.

2 

 3

4. Use the flower as an exotic garnish.

5. Fill the cups with any filling of your choice. Those in the picture have a creamy mashed potato filling, piped with a star nozzle, and sprinkled with nigella seeds.

 4

 5

Carrot

Carrots are versatile vegetables that can be eaten uncooked, steamed, boiled, braised, sautéed, caramelised, glazed, seared, grilled, puréed and pickled! They are now available throughout the year in most countries. Besides adding colour to food, carrots abound in nutritional goodness. They are an excellent source of vitamins A and B and calcium, and contain some sugar as well. There are several varieties of carrots growing in different parts of the world – the main ones are orange-red, red and black in colour. Orange-red carrots are the most common, and have a very dense texture. They are usually slender and long, and the inner core is just discernable. Red carrots have a distinctive yellow core, which is tougher than the red part. They look extremely colourful and decorative when cut into flowers, because of the natural colour contrast between the core and the outer portion. The third variety, the black carrot, is actually a dark purple-red, and has a bitter taste.

❊ TUBEROSES

1. Take a slender carrot. Scrape, trim and wash it. With a small, sharp knife, trim off the curved portions, about $1\frac{1}{2}$" away from the base, from the four sides: top, bottom, left and right, giving the base of the carrot a square tapered shape.

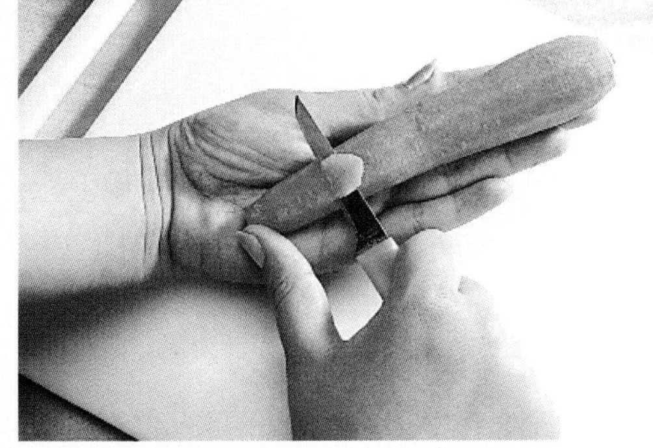

1

2

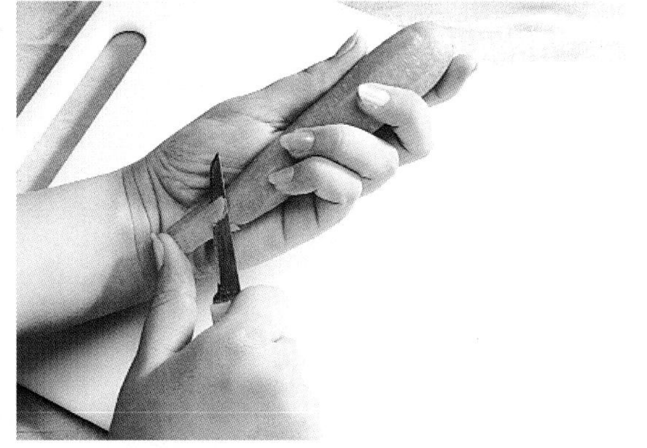

3

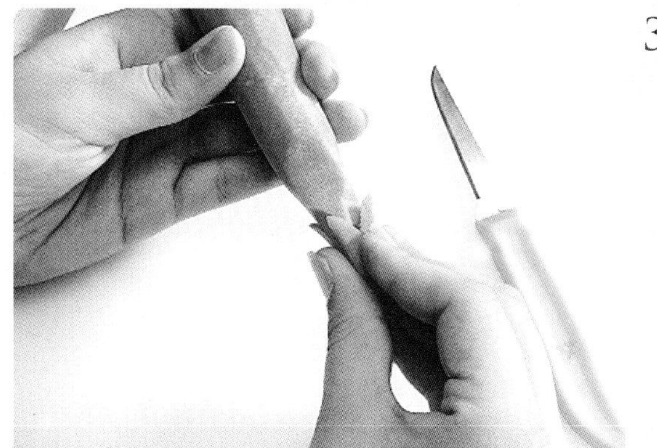

2. Then make a sharp angled cut, starting from the top of a squared corner, about 1/2″ downwards and inwards. Make similar cuts from the remaining three corners – all the cuts should meet at the base.

4

3. Hold the top of the carrot with one hand, and the base with the other. Break off the top portion. You will have a tuberose in one hand and the remaining part of the carrot in the other. Trim the square corners of the tuberose to a round shape, and the petals to an uniform size.

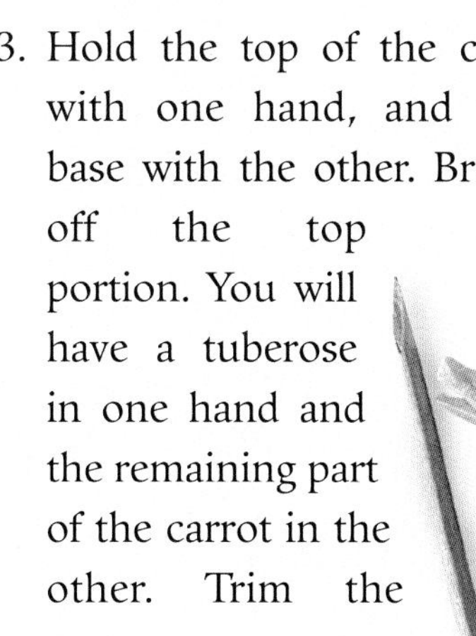

4. Continue this process till you have as many flowers as you need. Keep them in ice-cold water till they are required.

❊ CARROT FLOWERS

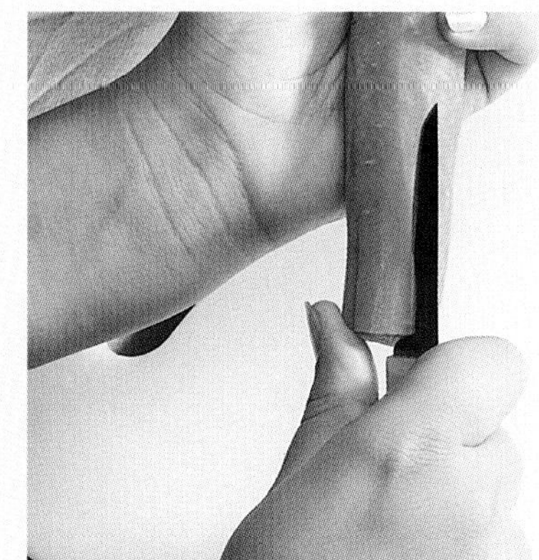

1

1. Scrape and wash a medium-sized carrot. Cut off the ends. Mark five equidistant notches around the lower end. With a small, sharp knife, make v-shaped grooves, about 1/8" deep, down the length of the carrot, starting from the notches.

2

2. When all the five grooved channels have been carved out, lay the carrot on its side on a chopping board. Cut slices in flower shapes, and keep them in ice-cold water until they are required.

Note: If you have a cannel knife, use it to carve the grooves.

1

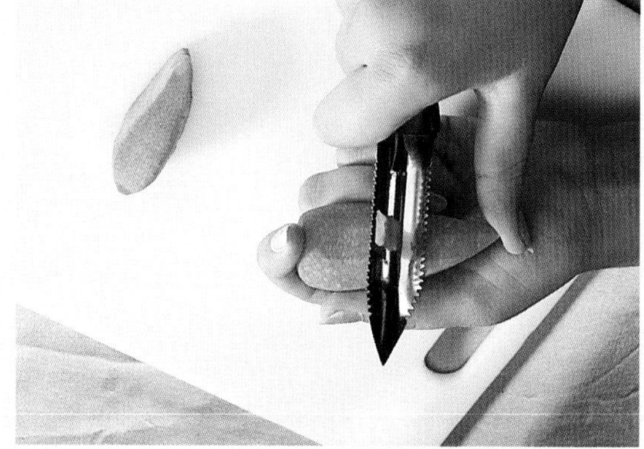

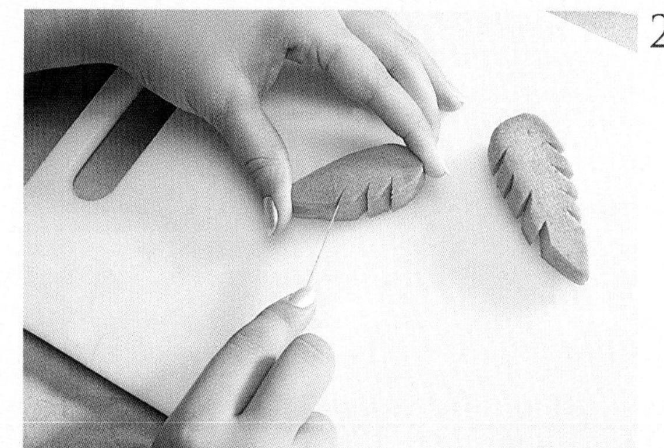

2

❊ CARROT FEATHERS

1. Depending on the size of the carrot, cut it into 2 or 3″ pieces. Trim both the ends and cut off a long slice from two opposite sides, making the carrot flat. With a sharp knife, round off the broader ends of the pieces, and taper the narrower ends to a point. Flatten them a little on the sides with a knife or peeler.

2. Lay carrot on a chopping board and cut out three or four v-shaped notches at an angle on both sides.

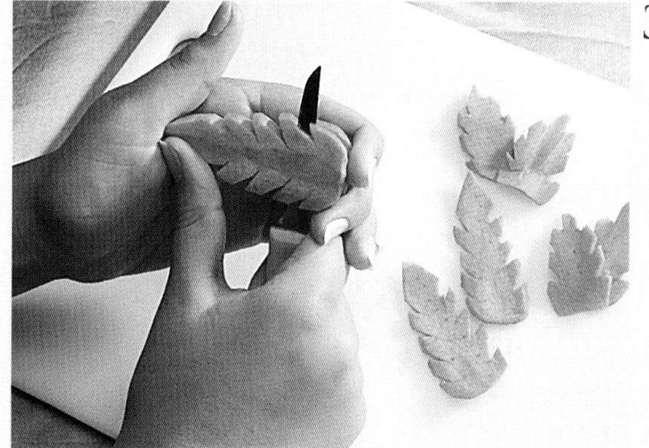

3

3. With a small knife, cut out thin slices along the length of the carrot. This will give you several feather shapes. Use them as required. If arranged in a circle, they form a big flower.

❊ ORIENTAL SALAD

Serves: 4

Ingredients

2 carrots
1 egg
1 cup bean sprouts
2 cups cabbage, finely shredded
1 cup spring onions, shredded

For the dressing:

2 tbsp oil
2 tbsp dark soya sauce

2 tbsp oyster sauce
2 tbsp vinegar
1 tbsp sugar
1/2 tsp garlic, ground
1/2 tsp ginger, ground
salt and pepper to taste

For the garnish:

a few slices of baby corn
a few carrot tuberoses
a few tender spring onion leaves

Method

1. Mix all the dressing ingredients several hours before assembling the salad. Keep covered in a cool place, stirring from time to time. (A screw-topped jar is best for this.)
2. Grate the carrots with the fine blade of a mandolin cutter – they should look like vermicelli. Otherwise, shred them into fine juliennes. Keep them in iced water.
3. Beat the egg with a pinch of salt. Heat a little oil in a pan; pour the beaten egg into it and lower the heat. Rotate the pan so that the egg is cooked properly inside. The moment it starts to set, roll it up tightly. Remove it from the heat. When the omelette is cool, cut it into thin slices.
4. In a bowl, toss the carrots, bean sprouts and omelette slices lightly.
5. Add the dressing and toss again.
6. Arrange the cabbage on a platter and pile the salad on it.
7. Arrange a spray of carrot tuberoses with the carrots, using spring onion greens in place of the leaves.
8. Place slices of baby corn all around the dish and serve.

Cucumber

A crisp and crunchy green vegetable that looks like a marrow, the cucumber is the mainstay of many salads. An almost indispensable part of summer salads, it is extremely low in calories and is a dieter's delight! Cucumbers have a delicate flavour and combine well with other salad ingredients.

Cucumbers grow on creepers like marrows and gourds. Though there are several varieties of the vegetable available, the long smooth-skinned English cucumber is always a good buy. When selecting a cucumber, choose small to medium-sized ones, which are firm to the touch. The larger ones are usually heavily seeded. A variety of cucumbers called gherkins are pickled and sold, and used in salads and sandwiches, greatly enhance their taste.

Though cucumbers can be cooked and combined with several foods, they are usually a part of uncooked vegetable salads. Because of their mild flavour, they should not be smothered with dressing or spices, but served with lemon juice or a vinaigrette dressing.

❊ CUCUMBER CROWNS

1. Wash and dry a firm, green cucumber. Cut off the ends. Using a small, sharp knife, cut a zigzag pattern about $1\frac{1}{2}$" away from the end. Push the knife into the cucumber up to the centre only, at an angle, then cut again in

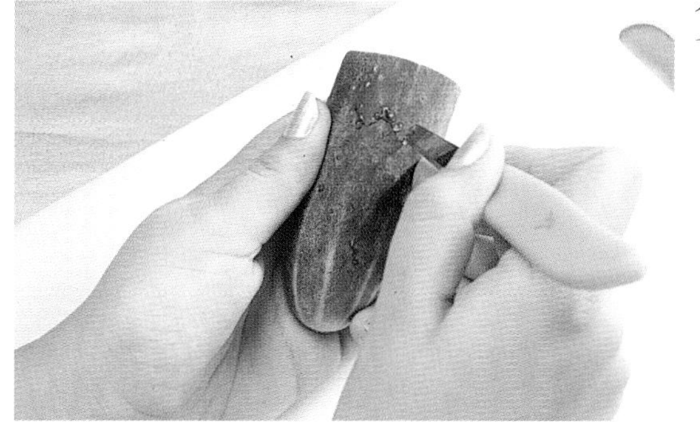

1

2

3

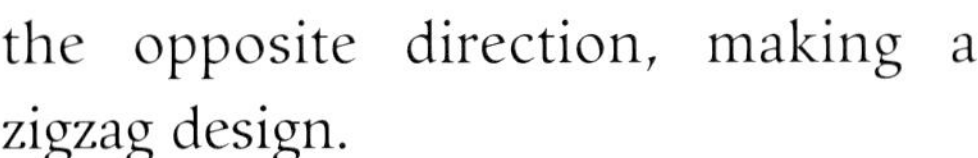

the opposite direction, making a zigzag design.

2. Prise the cut part away from the main cucumber.

3. Cut the cucumber again, 1½″ away from the zigzag edge. You now have two pieces that are flat on one end and serrated on the other. Cut as many pieces as you like. Using a corer, take out the seeds, leaving a hollow crown.

4. Fill with cream cheese or any filling of your choice, and serve it as an hors d'oeuvre.

✻ CUCUMBER FANS

1

1. Take a firm medium-sized cucumber. Ensure that it is not full of seeds. Cut it into 2 or 2½″ pieces. Cut two slices from opposite sides (about ½ to ¾″ thick), with the skin. Discard the inner

2

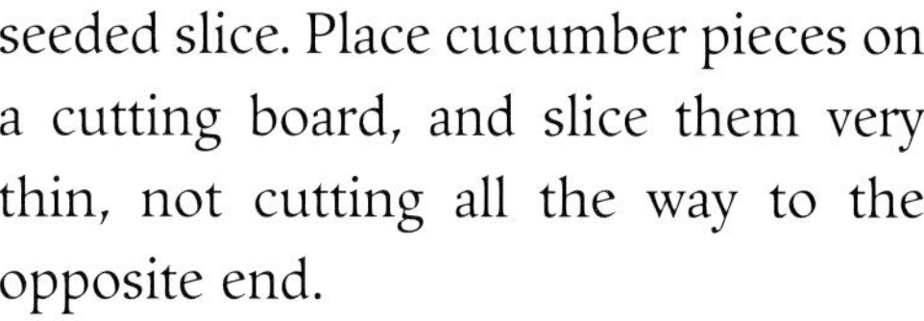

seeded slice. Place cucumber pieces on a cutting board, and slice them very thin, not cutting all the way to the opposite end.

3

2. Fold every alternate slice in a loop inside two unfolded ones.

3. Chill and use as a garnish.

❊ COOL CUCUMBER CHEESECAKE

Serves: 8

Ingredients

For the base:

- 175 gm salted biscuits, coarsely crushed
- a little pepper
- 75 gm butter
- 1 tbsp lemon juice

For the filling:

- 1/2 cucumber, coarsely grated
- a pinch of salt
- 1 tbsp gelatine
- 3 tbsp water
- 2 eggs, separated
- 1 tsp lemon rind
- 225 gm cream cheese

125 ml sour cream
2 cloves garlic, crushed
1 tbsp mint, finely chopped
salt and pepper

For the garnish:
lettuce leaves, chopped
tomato, sliced
mint leaves, chopped
2 cucumber fans (see p. 73)

Method

1. For the base, mix the pepper with the biscuit crumbs and rub in the butter. Sprinkle lemon juice and mix thoroughly. Press this mixture lightly on the base of a lined, loose-bottomed, 8″ cake tin, and chill it in a freezer while preparing the cheesecake.
2. For the filling, mix the cucumber with salt and leave it aside for half an hour. Then put it in a muslin cloth and squeeze dry. Ensure that all the liquid is squeezed out.
3. Soak gelatine in water in a small heatproof bowl. Let it stand for a few minutes, then place it over a bowl of hot water for a few minutes till it melts.
4. Beat the egg yolks over hot water with the lemon rind. Remove and add it to the gelatine. Mix well.
5. Blend the cream cheese and sour cream together with the garlic, mint, salt and pepper. Stir in the cucumber, and lastly the egg yolk mixture.
6. Beat the egg whites till stiff and fold it into the cream cheese mixture. Pour over the prepared base and chill, covered, till set.
7. To serve, turn out the cheesecake on a large serving platter. Surround with lettuce leaves, tomato and mint.
8. Place two cucumber fans and some mint leaves on top of the cheesecake and serve.

Ribbons and Curls

To cut vegetable ribbons, you will need a fine slicer on the mandolin cutter. Keep the vegetable flat , so as to get the maximum length while slicing it.

To make curls, take a ribbon of vegetable, and starting from the tapering end, roll it up tightly. Fix it firmly with a toothpick and place it in iced water till it is required. Vegetable curls can be served with dips.

Mushroom

When we talk about mushrooms, we usually refer to the white button ones that are commonly cultivated and eaten. These delicate fungi, however, belong to a vast family that grows and flourishes all over the world in pastures and woodlands. Some of them are highly regarded in gastronomic circles, but many are poisonous. It is easy to mistake the deadly *amanita verna* mushroom for the common edible field variety.

However, you cannot go wrong with the commercially grown button mushroom which adds a subtle flavour to any dish. Mushrooms can be fried, baked, sautéed and grilled; they can be pickled and preserved in oil; the large ones can be stuffed and cooked, and the small ones eaten raw in salads.

Mushrooms have a high water content and are low in calories. Many dried varieties are sold in the market – dried and powdered mushrooms make a tasty addition to any dish. Fresh mushrooms are very delicate, and they bruise and discolour easily.

✻ TURNED MUSHROOMS

1

1. With the tip of a small knife, mark the cap of a mushroom from the centre, outwards to the edge – this can be in a straight line or in a spiral. Make the cut a little deeper, about 1/4" towards the outer edge.

2. Now repeat the procedure, holding the knife at a slight angle, about 1/8 to 1/4" away., making a notch. Remove the cut piece. Continue like this all around the mushroom till the cap is totally grooved. Brush with lemon juice and use as required.

Note: These mushrooms, with spiral grooves carved on them, look very attractive as garnish on a salad. Mushrooms discolour very quickly, so carve them just before they are required, and brush them with lemon juice.

✻ MUSHROOM BASKETS

Serves: 4

Ingredients

8 mushrooms, large
4 spring onions, very thin
1 tbsp oil
1 tomato, medium, chopped
1 tbsp parsley, chopped
4 tbsp chicken or ham (optional), chopped, cooked
salt and pepper to taste

Method

1. Firmly break off the stems of the mushrooms. Trim and chop them.
2. Keep aside a few leaves, and chop the remaining spring onions with leaves.
3. With a small knife, cut away the rounded inner edges of the mushrooms. Mix the pieces whch were kept aside, with the chopped stems.

3

4

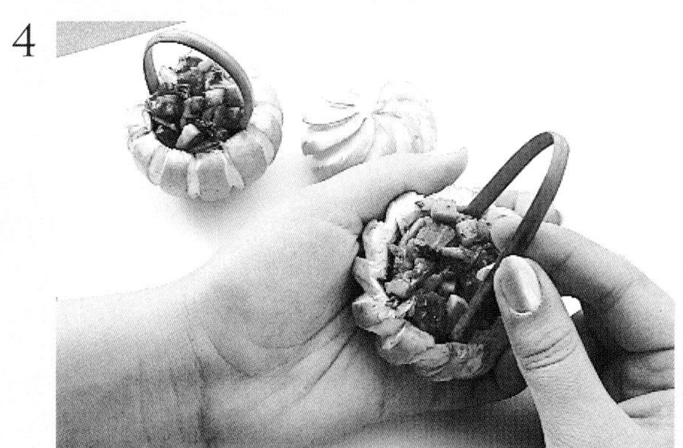

This will create more room for the stuffing, and make the basket look more natural.

4. Heat the oil in a frying pan, and sauté spring onions. Add tomato and mushroom stems. Cook them for a minute. Add parsley, chicken or ham, and seasonings, and cook till it is heated right through. Remove and keep warm.
5. Brush the pan with a little oil, and place the mushroom baskets in it, hollow sides down. Cook them for a minute or two.
6. Then turn them over and cook them till they are heated through – they should not be overcooked.
7. Remove from heat and spoon in the filling. Trim onion greens (which were kept aside), and insert them into the filling, so that they resemble basket handles. Serve hot.

Onion

The common onion, or the *allium cepa,* belongs to the lily family. It is hard to find a resemblence between onions and lilies, because usually the beautiful pompom-like onion flowers are ignored, and we only visualise the onion as a smelly but necessary vegetable that is indispensable in most kitchens.

Onions are known as spring onions when they are tiny bulbs, when the plant is small. In this form they emanate a crisp but mild onion flavour, and the greenish portion adds colour to any dish. The leaves taste like chives and are a good substitute for them.

Onions, on the other hand, are the mature bulbs of the dried plant, and can last for several weeks, if properly stored. They are of different sizes, and the inner layers can range from pure white to yellow to a purplish hue. They are usually round, but there are some elongated varieties. Though the vitamin content of the onion is modest, it is supposed to have stimulant properties for the intestines. It is also a diuretic.

✳ SPRING ONION TUBEROSES

1. Take a spring onion that does not have a rounded bulb. Trim off the leaves and the roots, cutting 1/2″ below the roots.

2. Slice thinly in one direction, as close as possible, making the cuts about 1″ deep.

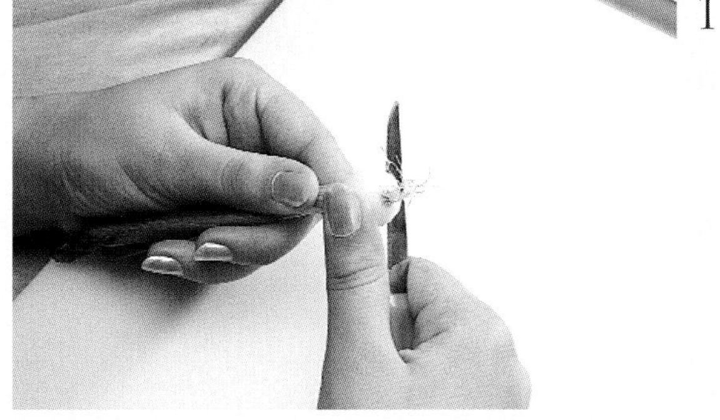

2

3

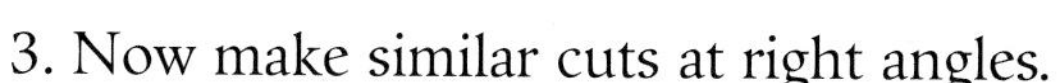

3. Now make similar cuts at right angles.

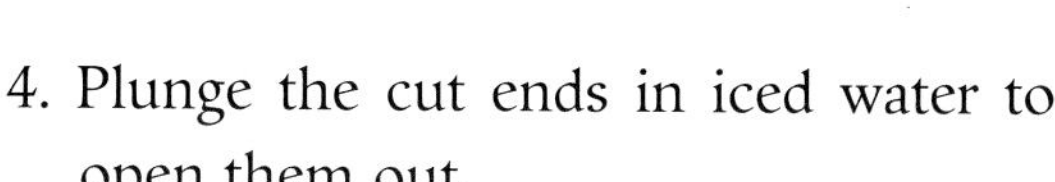

4. Plunge the cut ends in iced water to open them out.

5. Use as required as garnishing.

Note: If you cut the spring onion from the green side, you will get fronds.

1

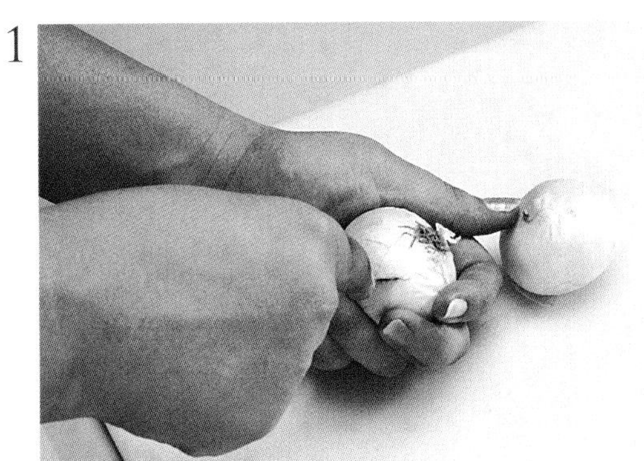

2

❊ BLUE LOTUS

1. Take a walnut-sized white onion with the skin on. With a small, sharp knife, cut in a zigzag fashion all around the widest part. Push the knife in up to the centre only.

2. Firmly prise the two halves apart.

3. Remove the skin, and trim away the root and stem ends.

4. Neaten the zigzag cuts.

5. Place in iced water to which blue food colouring has been added, until they are required.

3

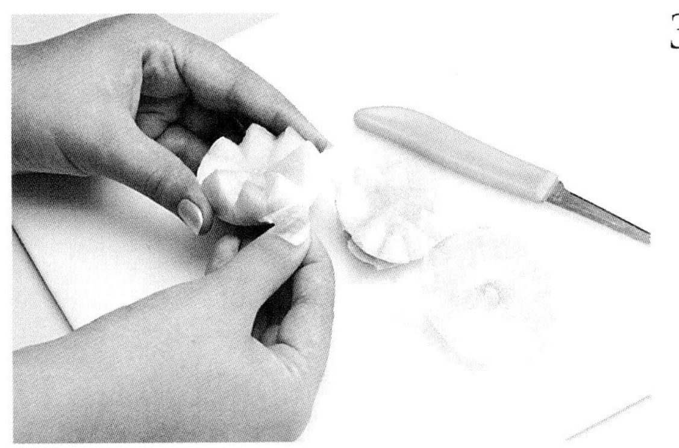

4

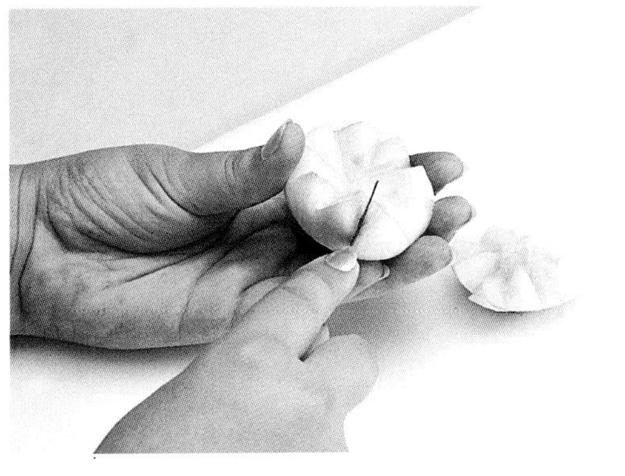

6. Remove the inner layers of the onion (use them to make buds), keeping three or four outer layers. Turn these into each other, so that the 'petals' look staggered. Use small vegetable balls as centres.

7. Use the exotic blue lotus flowers to decorate platters.

5

Pumpkin

Fat, flat, round, oval, smooth, knobbly, long and crooked – pumpkins come in many shapes, colours, sizes and varieties. If several kinds of these interesting-looking vegetables are placed together, they make a unique and colourful display. The American Halloween pumpkin is well known. It is carved, lit up, and placed on doorsteps all over America at Halloween. American pumpkin pie is as famous. The crisp orange flesh of a pumpkin can be used in both sweet and savoury dishes. It can be made into a soup, baked, puréed, or carved as a decoration piece for a buffet or banquet table. Large pumpkins can be carved into punch or soup bowls.

Pumpkins belong to the melon family, along with gourds and squashes. They grow in all the warm regions of the world. Some varieties contain up to 95 per cent water, with small amounts of carbohydrate.

❊ PUMPKIN BOWL

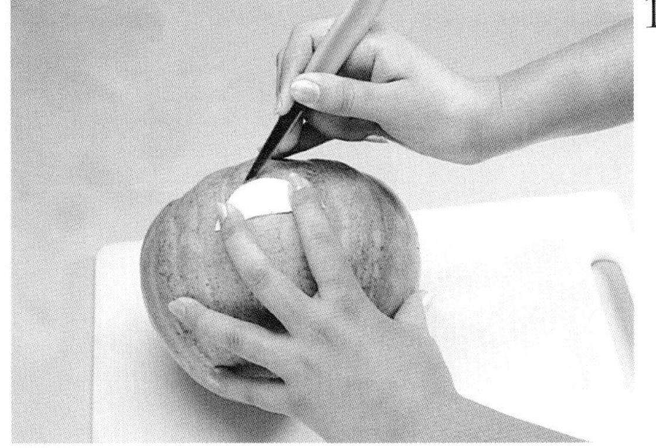

1. Make a scallop-shaped template of paper with a $1\frac{1}{2}$″-wide base. Place this template on a small and firm pumpkin, close to the stem end, and mark out the outline with a small knife. Repeat the marking all around the pumpkin.

2

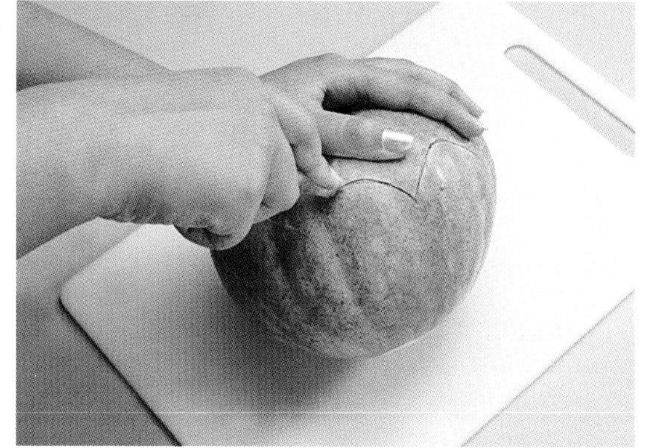

3

2. Then, still using a small, sharp knife, cut firmly through along the scalloped markings, holding the knife at a slight angle.

3. Prise the two pieces apart carefully, so that they are not damaged.

4. Scoop out the seeds with a spoon.

5. Using an x-acto cutter or a linoleum knife, make decorative grooves inside the scallops.

6. Then cut grooved lines at random in a

4

5

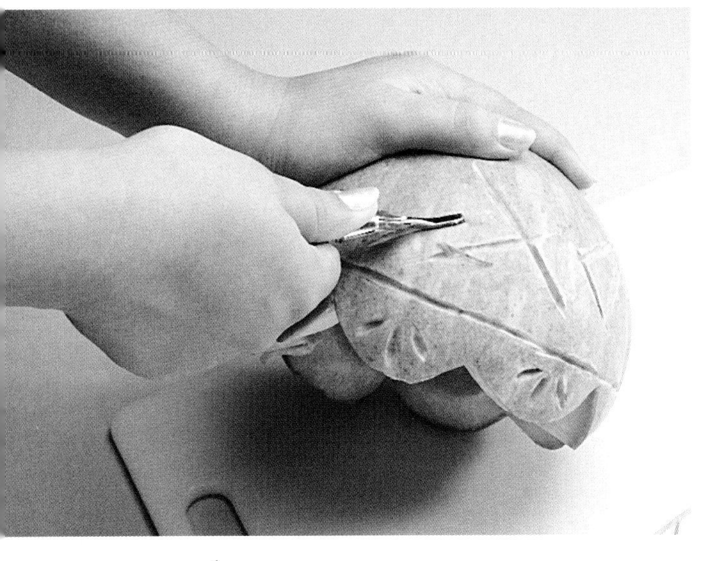

6

7

geometrical fashion, criss-crossing at some points.

7. With a small, sharp knife held almost flat, cut off pieces of rind from some of the shapes created by the grooved lines.

8. You can fill the bowl with spiced potatoes, as in the picture, or with any filling of your choice.

Red Radish

A pungent vegetable, radishes come in three main varieties. The most popular are the small round red ones – a peppery and colourful addition to salads. Then there are the long white variety, also called the daikon; and finally, the red and white globes.

Red radish is usually eaten raw in salads or as hors d' oeuvre. Its colour makes it attractive as a garnish. You can cut it in various shapes and then place it in ice water to open it out. White radish is good for making spaghetti, ribbons, cutouts; or it can be shaped into rolled or skewered flowers.

Radishes do not have great nutritional value, but they contain some vitamin C. They have, however, been used as an appetite stimulant since ancient times by the Romans, Egyptians and Chinese.

⁕ RED RADISH FLOWERS

1. Trim off the root end of the red radish. Make cuts, almost to the leaf end, about 1/8″ apart. Make similar cuts at right angles to these.

2. Place the radish in chilled water to open it out.

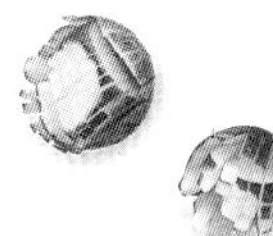

❊ RED RADISH LADYBIRDS

1

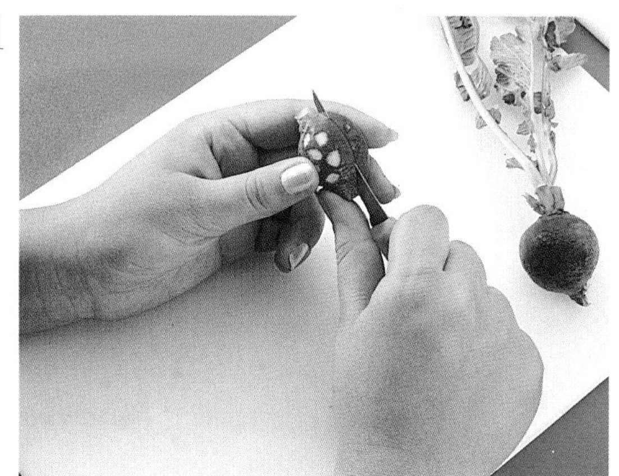

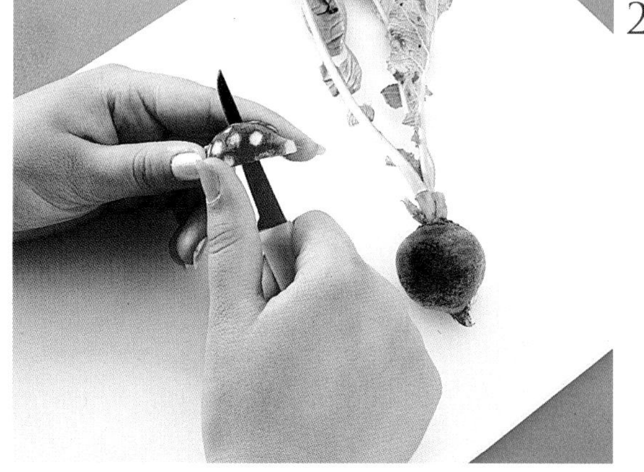

2

3

1. Trim off the root end of a red radish. Cut off the leaves, leaving a 1/4″ stub. Carve out tiny circles to resemble dots, and then slice the radish in half.

2. Cut again through the centre, from root end to the leaf end, leaving that end uncut.

3. Place it in iced water to open it out.

1 

 2

3 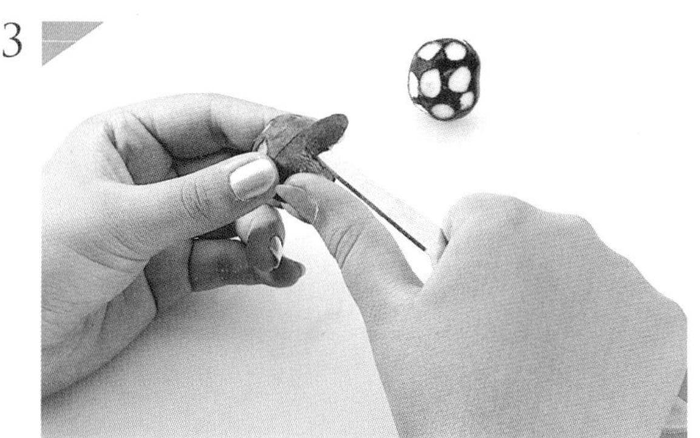

 4

❊ RED RADISH MUSHROOMS

1. Trim the root end of a red radish. Cut out tiny circles, resembling dots, from the broader side.

2. Make a 1/2″-deep cut all around the widest part of the radish.

3. Now make a cut at right angles to this, cutting off a stem shape below the 1/2″ cut you made in step 2.

4. Trim the 'stem' and level its base.

5. Place in iced water till required.

Ice Bowl

The perfect centrepiece for a summer feast

What is required

2 steel or plastic bowls
Ice cubes
Ice cold water
Mint leaves
Vegetable flowers
A heavy can or weight to weigh the inner bowl down.

Method

1. One bowl should be at least 2″ smaller in diameter than the other.
2. Place some ice cubes in the bigger bowl in a layer, to cover the base. Pour some water into it and place it in the freezer till the water is frozen, forming a layer that is just more than 1″ thick.

3. Remove from freezer and place smaller bowl on the frozen ice layer. Weigh this down with a heavy can or any other weight. Make sure that the inner bowl is in the centre and equal space is left all around between the bowls.
4. Place some vegetable flowers and leaves in this space, all around. Push down with the handle of a spoon.
5. Pour ice-cold water up to the top between the two bowls. Carefully place them in the freezer till the water becomes ice.
6. Take out from the freezer and remove the weight. Pour slightly warm water into the centre of the bowl and remove the inner bowl. Turn the bigger bowl with the ice bowl inside upside down. Wring out a towel in hot water and place it over the bowl – the ice bowl will come out easily.
7. Place it back in the freezer till required. It makes a wonderful bowl for a cool crisp fruit or vegetable salad, or to display frosted fruits.

Tomato

The tomato is the soft, pulpy fruit of a plant that is native to South America. It went from there to almost all parts of the world, and is one of the most widely grown and popular vegetables. Green when unripe, the tomato changes in colour to a vivid red when ripe. Its taste varies from bland to tart to sour. Besides adding an appetising taste and colour to soups, salads, curries, it is made into chutneys, pickles and sauces. It is salted, powdered, canned, puréed, or made into pastes. Tomatoes are perhaps the most versatile and commercialised food product in the world.

They are a good source of vitamin C. Therefore they are a good vegetable to include in one's daily diet. Tomatoes are a hot favourite as a garnish, and can be cut into slices, containers, baskets, flowers and rings. But since they are pulpy, they cannot be cut into shapes. Nevertheless, their colour and flavour makes them a sure winner always.

✻ TOMATO ROSE

1. Take a very firm and red tomato. Beginning at the stem end, start cutting the skin as though you were peeling it in a long strip. The strip should be as long as possible, as thin as possible, and about 3/4″ to 1″ wide. If it breaks, keep the broken part aside for use later on, and continue cutting.

1 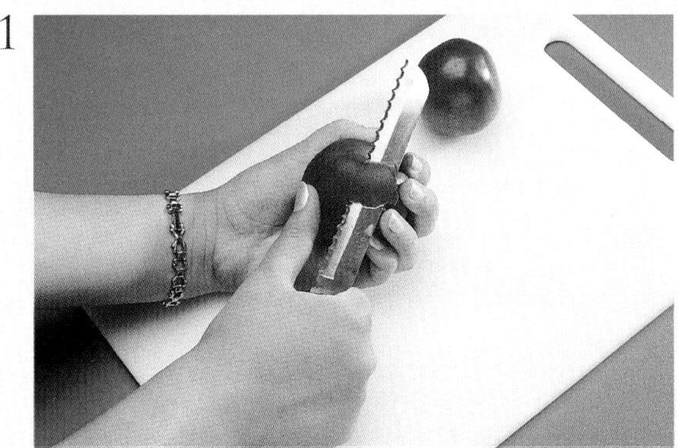

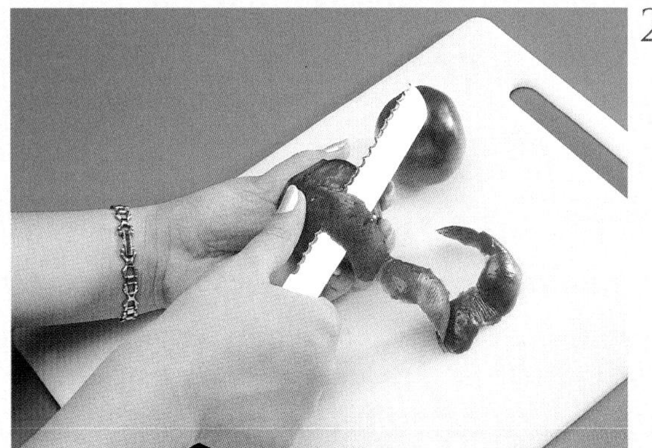 2

2. Now start rolling up the strip firmly. If it is broken, roll it up to the broken end, and place the other part of the strip over the rolled peel. Continue rolling it.

3. The tomato strip should now look like a real rose.

4. Make as many tomato-peel roses as you want, and use them as a garnish.

 3

❊ HOT CRUNCHY SALAD

Serves: 4

Ingredients

2 tomatoes, cut into thin slivers, deseeded
4 slices of stale bread
3 tbsp olive oil
2 cloves garlic, crushed
1 zucchini, thickly sliced
2 cups cabbage, finely shredded
1/2 cup onion greens, chopped

For the dressing:
1 tsp dried basil
1/4 cup olive oil
salt and pepper to taste
2 tbsp vinegar

For the garnish:
2 tomato flowers
a few spring onion greens

Method

1. For the dressing, mix all the ingredients together, store in a bottle, and keep till required.
2. Brush the stale slices of bread lightly with some olive oil. Then break it into bite-size chunks and put them in a hot oven to 'brown' them all over.
3. Before serving, heat the remaining oil, add the garlic, and cook it for a minute.
4. Add the zucchini and cook it for a few seconds more. Add the cabbage and toss well. Remove from heat and add the tomatoes to it.
5. Now toss in the bread pieces and the onion greens. Pour the dressing over this and mix well. Pile the salad on a plate.
6. Garnish with tomato flowers and onion greens and serve.

Zucchini

Zucchini, or courgette as it is also called, is a vegetable that looks rather like a cucumber. It is the fruit of herbaceous plants that grow to several feet in length. Though the smooth-skinned variety is the most common, there are other kinds of zucchini, which are round, oval or variegated.

Zucchini has a mellow flavour and is best eaten when it is still small. It can be used raw in salads, baked or fried. Baby zucchini is eaten whole, whereas the larger-sized ones are cut. The most popular zucchini dish is ratatouille. The flowers are stuffed and fried to make exotic dishes., and tender flowers, shoots and leaves are served sautéed with garlic and chilly.

Zucchini is a diuretic and a remedy for constipation. It is easily digestible, and its low calorie content makes it an ideal food for dieters.

⁕ ZUCCHINI FLOWERS

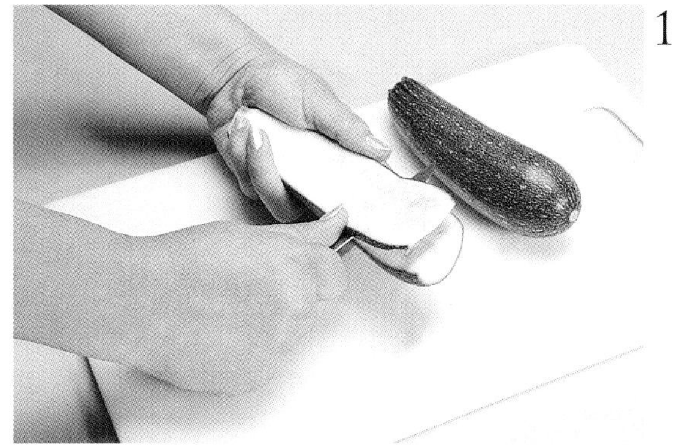

1

1. Cut thin slices of zucchini all along its length.

2. Cut off one side, along the length, to give it a straight edge. This will also make it easier to roll it into a flower. Then make cuts, 1/8″ apart, about 1″ in

2

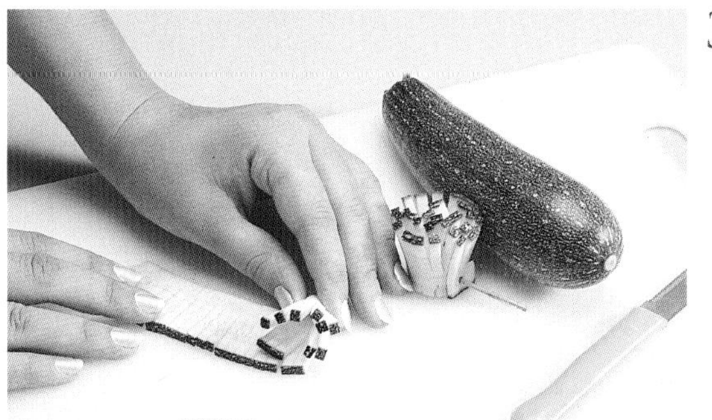

3

length, all along the strip, cutting from the edge, with the skin, towards the edge which was trimmed.

3. Starting from one end, roll it up firmly. Push a toothpick through the base to hold the zucchini flower in place.

4. To make the flowers stand out, cut out leaves from a cabbage, arrange them to look like a bowl, and place the zucchini flowers in them.